# debbie travis'
# painted house
# kitchens
# &baths

more than 50 innovative projects for an
exciting new look at any budget

*Debbie Travis with Barbara Dingle*
*Main Photography by George Ross*

Clarkson Potter / Publishers
New York

# debbie travis' painted house
# kitchens &baths

Copyright © 2003 by Debbie Travis

Main photography copyright © 2003 by George Ross. Step-by-step photography copyright © 2003 by Ernst Hellrung.

Please see page 173 for additional photography credits.

Published by Clarkson Potter/Publishers, New York, New York. Member of the Crown Publishing Group, a division of Random House, Inc.
www.randomhouse.com

CLARKSON N. POTTER is a trademark and POTTER and colophon are registered trademarks of Random House, Inc.

Printed in Japan

Design by Jan Derevjanik

Library of Congress Cataloging-in-Publication Data
Travis, Debbie.
    Debbie Travis' painted house kitchens and baths : more than 50 innovative projects for an exciting new look at any budget / Debbie Travis with Barbara Dingle.—1st ed.
        p. cm.
    1. House painting—Amateurs' manuals.
2. Furniture painting—Amateurs' manuals.
3. Interior decoration—Amateurs' manuals.
I. Dingle, Barbara.   II. Title.
    TT323 .T6924    2003
    747.7'97—dc21                              2002155158

ISBN 0-609-80549-5

10  9  8  7  6  5  4  3  2  1

First Edition

*To my mom, who created my happiest childhood memories in her kitchen.*

# acknowledgments

Whether you are renovating or decorating your home by yourself or with the help of professionals, it is always a team effort, especially in a kitchen and a bathroom.

Just like you, I am not alone as I undertake about thirty makeovers a year. I have so much incredible help from my team behind the scenes. There are now two television shows, *Debbie Travis' Painted House* and *Debbie Travis' Facelift*. It is the painters, artists, carpenters, stylists, and photographers who make these shows and this book possible. I would like to hug them all.

First, I must thank my art directors and designers, Anne Coté, Alison Osborne, and Mazyar Mortazavi, who help orchestrate the whole design process. The painters and artists whose talents are unsurpassed are Sue Pistawka, Andrejs Ritins, Lynn Roulston, James Simon, Paul Shivkumar, Hubert Simard, Stephanie Robertson, Pauline Saint-Armand, Melanie McSpurren, Beata Nawrocki, Ben Roberts, Elena Hattersley, Travis Champion, Joseph Brady and Alison Sharpe. The brilliant and speedy carpenters and contractors are Reg Clarke and his team, and Ian Butzphal, Allone Koffkinsky, Paul Vernon, R. J. Pickering, Francis O'Keefe and Rick Thompson. When the rooms are all finished, I owe a big debt of gratitude to Valorie Finnie, Elaine Miller, and Paola Ridolfi, who dress the spaces so beautifully.

It takes a special eye to photograph a room, and I am indebted to George Ross, who makes every space look stunning. Thank you to the other photographers who have added their skills to my book: Ernst Hellrung for the step-by-steps and Brigitte Bruyez, Joe Oliveira, and Peter Sellar for their contributions.

Once the rooms are finished and the photography is in hand, the writing begins. Thank you to Barbara Dingle, who continues to write along with me, exhibiting her trademark patience and skill no matter how tight the deadlines. Thanks to Janice Kaluza for all her careful research. And a huge thank you to Dana MacKimmie, who organizes the whole team—a scary job!

There would be no book without the dedicated enthusiasm of my editor, Annetta Hanna. And thanks also to Marysarah Quinn and Jan Derevjanik, whose fabulous layouts show off each kitchen and bathroom.

My heartfelt thanks go to all the homeowners who were brave enough to let us redesign their kitchens and bathrooms. And the biggest thanks of all go out to my television audience and readers around the world. It is your excitement, tuning in every week to watch each episode of *The Painted House* and *Facelift*, buying my books and reading my syndicated newspaper column, that makes everyone's hard work so rewarding. Thank you all.

# contents

## kitchen and bathroom makeovers

# preface

I have helped to design countless rooms for friends, clients, and for my television shows *The Painted House* and *Facelift*, but when decisions must be made for my own home, the process is nothing short of painful. In the last eighteen months, I have designed, renovated, and decorated my kitchen and master bathroom. Both rooms were enormous jobs and consequently expensive, time consuming, and disruptive to everyday family life. This may sound disheartening if you are about to embark on your own kitchen or bathroom makeover, but please do not misunderstand me; the results far outweigh the months of renovation. I look back on that hectic time in the same way a mother looks at childbirth. Yes, the birth was painful, but the memory fades fast when you gaze on your new baby. It's the same with a renovation of this magnitude. When I sit in my new kitchen surrounded by friends, watch over a child as he studies, or take a delicious soak in my own private spa, I am filled with a sense of delight.

The renovation process is a constant lesson, and one that begins with the importance of planning. Even if you have the help of an architect and a designer, learn to ask questions and be there for every decision. You will probably not build a new kitchen or bathroom many times in your lifetime; therefore it is imperative to create a space that fits your ever-evolving lifestyle and maximizes how you use the budget. When the work begins, so does your alternative lifestyle: the camping out in the dining room, washing the dishes in the bathtub, and getting to know the local takeout very well. Stay focused, and I promise you that before you know it, you will be thriving in your new kitchen and bathroom.

My kitchen is the hub of the house—
my favorite place to chat with friends.

# introduction

There are no other rooms in the home that impact our lives quite like the kitchen and bathroom. I chose to team these two rooms together in one book because they have so much in common. They are utilized in vastly different ways but the elements that make up both the kitchen and the bathroom are closely related. They each have fixtures and fittings, cabinetry, countertops, and flooring that need to be water resistant and easy to clean. They are also the costliest and most time consuming rooms in the home to make over, whether you are just refinishing the cupboard doors or treating yourself to all new appliances. The commitment of time and money, if well spent, will be a good investment for years to come.

There is another reason that these two rooms are so similar. Today the roles of the kitchen and bathroom have extended far beyond their traditional functions. Until recently, the kitchen was simply the place where food was stored, prepared, and eaten. It is now the center of the home, a gathering place for family and friends. It forms a backdrop for everyday living: chatting on the phone, doing homework, watching TV, catching up with friends, and sharing stories at the end of the day.

The bathroom has evolved even more than the kitchen. Early bathrooms were functional spaces with hot water as a luxury. It wasn't until after World War I that the average North American home was given proper plumbing. Prior to that, toilets were at the back of the yard and bath time usually entailed a weekly scrub in a tin bath in front of the kitchen range. Since the 1960s the availability of new materials enabled bathrooms to have the design elements of style and color. But it is only in the last decade that bathrooms have become as exciting a part of the home as any other room. The explosion of the "spa experience" has given new dimensions to personal bathing. The modern bathroom is now therapeutic, a place to prepare to face the day or to relax before bed. Inspiration is derived from other cultures where bathing has always been a ritual, drawing upon the history of grandly painted Roman baths, elaborately tiled Turkish baths, or simple Scandinavian saunas to re-create the art of unrushed bathing.

The renovation of the kitchen and bathroom is a journey of planning, preparation, and good budgeting, whether you are starting from scratch or just changing the color of the kitchen cabinets. Successful results come from using the right materials—the correct stone for the tops of your kitchen counters, the right primer to enable you to paint over the old wood cabinets. In the following pages you will find ideas for brand new kitchens and bathrooms. But if your budget does not accommodate starting from scratch, then there are also many ways to design a new look without the cost. You may also be renting and just want to update the space with a splash of color. Follow all the step-by-step instructions at the back of the book, plan well, and most of all enjoy the challenge.

# strictly cosmetic

The simplest and least expensive route to a new look is to make a cosmetic change. Paint and premixed plaster can renew walls, cabinets, and even countertops for a quick facelift that will transform even the shabbiest surroundings. If you can't change the permanent fixtures, then create an eye-catching finish on the paintable surfaces. This is the most popular path for renters, or if you have just bought a house or condominium and have little left over in the kitty. Look at the magical change to the loft kitchen on page 70, where bold bands of green and blue paint have been rolled onto the cabinets and backsplash area. Color has revitalized a bland but modern kitchen. In the bathroom called French Twist on page 110, a plaster technique applied over the existing tile has transformed a '70s standard bathroom into a little corner of Provence. Many of these surfaces are shiny, so it is imperative to follow all the preparation and sealing steps for long-lasting results.

# a bit of both

The next level of improvement involves making both cosmetic and larger changes. You have decided to replace one or two appliances such as the kitchen stove or the bathtub, even put in new countertops or a new floor, but the layout of the space will remain the same. The challenge will be how to combine the new and the old. If you are replacing the sink but not the toilet, or just the stove, keep in mind that colors, including white, will differ from one manufacturer to the next, and from one year to the next; matching them may be a problem. Also, the dimensions of the new stove, refrigerator, sink, bathtub, or toilet may vary from those items they have replaced, so accurate measurements are necessary from the start. Once you have the new elements, then it's time to pick paint colors and accessories that will create a unified style. In the Retro Reno kitchen on page 66 the homeowner splurged on new stainless steel appliances, but the '70s-style white laminate cabinets had to stay. By painting them in tones of aqua I was able to produce the sleek modern kitchen the owner wanted at little cost.

When you change the period style of a kitchen or bathroom, display gadgets and accessories that complement the new look. Add appropriate design elements, such as a designer kettle, a sleek steel coffee maker, or some interesting bottles. In the bathroom, fill glass jars with beautiful soaps, decant shampoo and hand cream into decorative pump containers, and look for ceramic dishes designed to hold the toothpaste. Other necessities can be kept in cupboards until needed.

# starting from scratch

The most dramatic level of renovating is the complete makeover. If you have the budget and decide to build an entirely new kitchen or bathroom, it will be to your advantage to enlist the help of an architect or designer who specializes in these rooms. This is the road with the most options and perils. The variety of available products, layouts, colors, and styles is overwhelming. The evolution in the design of fixtures, fittings, and materials for the kitchen and bathroom is enormous and exciting. Designers and manufacturers have flooded the market with choices for every look and price range. But good kitchen and bath retailers have knowledgeable staff and useful tools such as computer programs to help you make wise and manageable decisions. Doing your homework will result in a renovation that will serve you well for years to come.

Whichever level of improvement you decide upon, take the time to learn what's available and determine what you really want. Visit showrooms and shops, browse the Internet, look through magazines and style books, and talk to the experts. Break down the kitchen or bathroom into its essential elements and recognize the role that each plays for you and how you live. If you spend a lot of time in the kitchen, the floor material should be warm, comfortable, and forgiving. If your counterspace is limited, maybe you can afford to splurge on slate, granite, or stainless steel. A family bathroom demands plenty of storage and easy-to-clean surfaces. A tiny powder room may be the perfect space to apply more difficult or costly finishes or to introduce a brave new style.

The following chapter will provide you with an overview of the essential elements that comprise the kitchen and bath, such as cabinetry, counters, flooring, fixtures, and fittings. The various materials used in making these products are listed along with their pros and cons. For each of the elements there is a guide to the possible makeover options if you want to renew rather than replace what you already have. Use this information as a jumping-off point for your research and then find out what is economical and available where you live.

The Kitchen and Bathroom Makeovers section invites you to explore real-life transformations. Here I have worked with the homeowners and their specific challenges to come up with kitchen and bathroom redesigns for *The Painted House* and *Facelift* television shows. The budgets and spaces vary greatly, but the results are always amazing. Step-by-step instructions accompany the projects that are unique to a room. Color is always a dominant concern, and I've added a chat box for each room called Color Conversation, which explains the distinct color palette chosen so that you can transfer the ideas to your own rooms.

Many surfaces, such as wood and laminate cabinets, tile countertops, and backsplash areas, are common to both kitchens and bathrooms, and so to avoid repetition, the instructions for how to prepare and resurface these are grouped together in the final chapter, Back for Basics. The most frequently asked questions are answered there, such as how to paint over laminate cabinets, tile, and even countertops. There are tips on the best paint products to use, and how to apply and seal plaster and concrete, one of the hot new materials for kitchens and bathrooms. We refer to this section throughout Kitchen and Bathroom Makeovers to connect you with the basic steps.

It is a delightful luxury to be able to dream up a new kitchen or bathroom. Be inspired by what you see and love. I hope this book will help you decide on a route to take and give you the means to get there.

# elements
## of the kitchen

The old notion of the kitchen being a hidden, separate room, the exclusive domain of the housewife, has disappeared over the last few decades. Kitchens today are public spaces that are seen and enjoyed by family and friends alike. As everyday living has taken over the kitchen, its shape and size have evolved and grown to keep up. First, eat-in kitchens absorbed the dining room, and now many kitchens have encroached onto the living room's activities as well. Today's open-plan houses and lofts reveal the kitchen as a multipurpose space, and even older homes have opened up their walls. This visibility means that the kitchen should be as stylish as the rest of the home.

But you cannot forget the kitchen's primary function. In order to enjoy your kitchen, it must work well. All the basic elements—appliances, cabinets, and lighting—must be considered first, as they will dominate the space. Choices for floors, countertops, sink and fixtures, furnishings, and color should follow. They embellish the style.

The materials that go into making up a kitchen have to be highly durable in order to withstand heat, moisture, and constant wear. They must also be hygienic and easy to clean and disinfect. Today's vast choices make it possible to get the hardworking materials you need along with the style you want. Plastic laminate countertops have come a long way since the original imitation--marble offerings and are now available in many colors. Products like Corian are tough and easily installed and have the smooth finish of granite. Old flooring products such as vinyl and linoleum are back in vogue, manufactured in lush colors and designs that range from retro to new age.

Whether you are starting from scratch or just want to give your kitchen a facelift, review the diversity of products and materials we present here. Then, knowing what you already have, decide if you want to improve what's there or start over. With today's marvelous high-adhesive paint primers and the improved durability of latex (water-based) paint, the makeover opportunities are limitless.

The kitchen is the most expensive room in the house to design, but what a joy it is when you get it right. Food storage, meal preparation, and the inevitable cleanups will seem less onerous when you create a space that makes you smile.

# cabinets and shelving

Storage space in the kitchen is essential for packaged and canned goods, dishes, cutlery and cooking utensils, as well as for the cookbooks, wine bottles, and countless other things that seem to collect in this area. Some people prefer to put away everything behind closed doors, while others like to combine closed storage with open shelves or glass-front cabinets that display their contents.

In a fitted kitchen all the cabinetry and appliances are set permanently in place. The cabinets may be solid faced, which gives a uniform look to the walls, or glass-fronted cabinets may be included, usually along the top. This style tends to open up the space and is just as appropriate in an old-fashioned country kitchen as a contemporary one. It's what lies behind the glass that sets the tone.

The freestanding, as opposed to fitted, kitchen is once again popular, although with a modern twist. This offers an interesting alternative to fitted cabinets, allowing old and new pieces of furniture and shelving to live happily together. A painted pine armoire can hold heavy items, while an old chest of drawers can be used for cutlery and linens. Industrial steel shelves can display piles of white plates. Support blocks can be used to ensure an even height for different pieces and a new countertop can create a continuous work surface. Freestanding pieces can be antique or new, or they can be custom built to fit your needs. As with fitted cabinets, details such as paint color, sheen and finish, and hardware will set the style.

Cabinets are usually constructed from a combination of materials; the interior or hidden parts are made of less costly plywood or fiberboard, and the outer surfaces or facings are made of wood or plastics or steel.

PREVIOUS PAGE: A small galley kitchen has been updated with the once-again popular subway tiles, vintage floor, and traditional cabinets.

Solid woods such as pine, oak, maple, or birch offer the intrinsic beauty of their color and grain and, with the proper care, will last a lifetime. Generally custom built, the cost of solid-wood cabinetry is high but represents a good investment. Factory-made painted wood cabinets allow you to choose from the full-color spectrum and are sprayed for a tough, durable finish.

Wood veneer is a thin layer of wood that is adhered to a solid but less costly wood base, offering the visual advantages of solid wood. However, veneers can split or lift, especially where moisture is present, and they are difficult, if not impossible, to repair.

Wood laminates are made by adhering thin layers of solid wood over compressed woods such as chipboard and fiberboard.

Fiberboard is made of compressed wood fibers. Medium-density fiberboard (MDF) has a smooth surface perfect for flat-faced finishes and is less costly than solid wood. MDF's density makes it heavy.

Plastic laminates such as melamine and vinyl make up the most common type of stock cabinetry on the market. These finishes, which can be tinted in solid colors or patterned to look like wood, are adhered to a chipboard or fiberboard base. They are tough and easy to wipe clean. But, like wood veneer, the thin coating can split, chip, or lift away from its base and is difficult to repair.

Thanks to the demand for contemporary design in the fast-growing commercial-building market, a new generation of funky laminates has been created. These are made from layers of patterned papers that are fused together under high pressure. They are available in every color and in a variety of patterns, including plain or patterned stainless steel.

Glass can be cut and hung as a door or drawer front or installed as an inset into a wood or laminate frame. Glass should always be tempered for safety, and the edges can be beveled. It comes in clear, opaque, colored, and etched styles and is impervious to stains. Since it is breakable, however, glass is best suited to upper cabinets or drawers that won't be banged about.

Metal cabinets will bring industrial chic to the kitchen. Metal in the kitchen is a growing trend and there are several types used, from zinc to copper. The most popular, though, is stainless steel. A thin metal sheet is wrapped around fiberboard and the corners are rounded to avoid sharp edges. A variety of finishes are available: polished, matte, brushed, and sandblasted. For a less expensive steel effect, see above about stainless steel–effect laminates.

CLOCKWISE, FROM TOP LEFT:
Citrus yellow laminated cabinets are a stunning complement to today's sleek kitchens.

Chicken wire inserted into cabinet doors produces instant country style.

Here practicality mixes well with the streamlined beauty of wood veneer.

When you are deciding whether to replace or reface existing cabinets, it is important to know what material they are currently made of. In most cases, refinishing is not only possible, but will allow you to totally redefine your kitchen's style and mood. The versatility of paint allows you to transform plain surfaces into what appear to be expensive materials. There's metallic paint, glazes, and marbling and stone techniques using water-based paints.

You cannot improve warped or badly split wood, but minor repairs are easily fixed with wood filler. Solid wood cabinets make excellent surfaces for any paint effect including plain color, colorwashing, distressing, stenciling, and stamping. Wood veneer or laminate is paintable as long as it is not damaged.

Plastic laminate cabinets can also be painted, but particular care must be taken when you are preparing the shiny surface (see page 148). Allow extra time for the high-adhesive acrylic primer and each coat of paint to dry.

The design of the doors will be your key to the cabinet's style. Flat-faced doors suit a contemporary kitchen, while doors with raised panels and moldings are dressier and more traditional. You can change the look of your cabinets by adding strips of stock molding to flat-faced doors, or reinvent them by cutting out sections of the upper cabinet doors and inserting glass.

A new finish deserves fresh hardware: Either repaint or clean up what is there or splurge on some new handles. The choices available are phenomenal today, ranging from whimsical motifs such as kettles and utensils to pretty

Textured metal fronts dress vertical cabinets and drawers in this distinctly contemporary design.

Pot racks are a traditional surface space saver.

painted ceramics to lean-lined chrome. For smaller budgets, buy stock wooden knobs and hand-paint or stain them. Imaginative alternatives include boat cleats or the hardware used to wrap the cord for blinds.

# appliances

The design, condition, and color of your appliances have a major impact on how your kitchen looks and works. Modern appliances are designed not only for function but also for style. Because so much has changed in the world of electronics within the last ten years, you may have a stove or refrigerator that still works but looks completely out of date. And options for today's appliances are almost limitless. All appliances come either as stand-alone items or as built-ins. There are drawer-size dishwashers and refrigerators, and freezers and fridges that resemble oversized armoires; microwaves can be hung under a cabinet; stovetops can be situated in an island in the middle of the room, and ovens can be placed in the wall. These versatile designs make kitchen planning more flexible, but also more complex.

Not only your budget, but also how you use your kitchen will dictate the size of your appliances and their options. Choose a refrigerator that's suitable for the number of people in your household. The stove should reflect the way you cook. Will you use six elements and two ovens? Additional small appliances like a food processor, toaster oven, coffeemaker and bread maker are a tremendous convenience for busy cooks. But if takeout or dining out is more your style, stick to the basics. Anything more is a needless expense.

## what's available

Stainless steel, once strictly a commercial material, is now standard for the modern home kitchen. At first the cool silver tones were seen in only the most contemporary settings. But stainless steel's tough, no-nonsense appearance has proven to be very versatile. Inspired by all the television cooking shows, we are now comfortable with stainless steel appliances including oversized fridges, dishwashers, wall ovens, stoves, and ranges. Stainless steel also blends well with every style of kitchen, from a simple country look, to the moldings of a more traditional style, to the sleek lines of modern designs.

Although brightly colored appliances in Chinese red, brilliant blue, and sunflower yellow are readily available in Europe, North American showrooms carry

RIGHT: Stainless steel stoves and refrigerators have moved from the restaurant into the home.

OPPOSITE: Appliances can be disguised with panels that coordinate with the kitchen's decor.

As kitchens take on the look of furnished rooms, dishwashers and refrigerators are housed in drawers or paneled in wood.

predominantly white or stainless steel products with some black and smoked-glass models. Perhaps the avocado green stoves and chocolate brown refrigerators of the '60s scared us away from color.

Over time, designs have been modified and become more compact. So if you are replacing appliances in a fitted kitchen, as is usually the case, be prepared to make some adjustments to the surrounding countertops and possibly cabinets.

## makeover opportunities

Major appliance manufacturers sell panels that can give older models an instant facelift. The panels allow you to customize the front facings of your appliances, and come in stainless steel, white, and veneers. Check with your local retailer to see if there are panels available for your make and model.

Because of the heat factor, I do not recommend you paint a stove, but you can paint a refrigerator. I have used metallic paint on fridges and it works well. You can also apply sticky-backed paper onto the door panels. These alternatives aren't meant to be more than stop gaps, but they will last for a few years.

## countertops and backsplashes

The kitchen counter is a busy place. It has to put up with the daily onslaught of spills, hot pots, knives, and packages. As a workstation for preparing food, it must be hygienic and sturdy. There should be space to house a food processor, a coffee maker, a toaster, and other equipment in regular use. The countertop material must be water resistant with well-sealed seams and edges, especially around the sink. Tough and resilient are the main priorities for counters but they must also be easy to keep clean. And, of course, since we are working on it or looking at it a great deal of the time, the counter should have eye-appeal. It is an integral part of the kitchen decor.

The backsplash is accurately named. It is the area that sits above the countertop and protects the wall from grease, water, steam, and food. The countertop and backsplash are often made from the same material but the backsplash can also be a decorative band of tile, a sheet of Plexiglas, or even several coats of high-gloss varnish that will protect the wall paint. These are materials that are scrubbable but not durable enough for the countertops.

From the tried-and-true choice of butcher blocks and ceramic tiles to the latest in solid surface materials, stainless steel, stone, and concrete, countertops and backsplashes offer great design possibilities. You may decide to mix and match different materials depending on function and budget. And there is no need to spend a fortune to get a magnificent look. Here are your options.

**Wood** Wood counters are once again growing in popularity since they fit equally well with high-tech designs and in traditional country kitchens. Wood contains a natural acidity that protects the surface from germs but it must be treated correctly before being installed so that it can withstand heat and moisture. Wood countertops can be damaged if heavy objects fall on them, so it's important to use a hard wood. Surfaces need to be maintained with an occasional oil treatment for protection and to enhance the color and grain. If a dishwasher is to be installed, then a vapor barrier should be glued to the underside of the wood counter to avoid warping.

Butcher block is made of strips of hardwood laminated together. Its no-nonsense rustic appeal is especially popular in country and cottage kitchens. Do not seal the wood if you intend to use the counter as a cutting surface. Clean it with a warm, damp cloth and detergent, and wipe up liquid spills quickly. Use sandpaper to remove tough stains.

**Plastic Laminate** If your kitchen was built within the past twenty years, the countertops are most likely made of a plastic laminate. This durable material comes in a wide range of solid colors, patterns such as faux marble and granite, and textures that imitate stone, but at a fraction of the cost. It's also easy to keep clean so it is no wonder it's a popular choice. But the plastic layer is quite thin and can scar and chip. Repairs are difficult, although there are kits available.

**Ceramic Tile** There is a tile to complement every kitchen. The price of decorative tiles can run high, but you need use only a few as accents, covering the rest of the surface with plain tiles. Border and edge tiles give you the freedom to design any number of wonderful patterns. Tiles also mix well with wood, a softer material that is more forgiving when something is dropped on it. Glazed tiles are water and stain resistant, but the grouting that surrounds the tiles takes some upkeep. Even when sealed, grout breaks down and stains after a few years, requiring touchups.

**Solid Surface** This material is a compound made from acrylic polymers and natural minerals. Custom fabricated to fit your kitchen, it is often installed in one piece; openings can be precut where needed for the sink and stovetop if you choose. Solid-surface counters are seamless, which gives them a clean, sweeping look, with no lines to separate or collect dirt. Minor scratches and burn marks can be buffed away. Available in matte and gloss finishes and in a wide range of colors, solid-surface colors can also emulate the look of granite and stone.

Butcher blocks were once used solely in country settings but they also blend well with modern solid countertops, such as Corian.

Dated laminate countertops can be given a fresh coat of paint; see page 148.

**Natural Stone** Marble and granite are traditionally the most popular stones for countertops and backsplashes. They are unquestionably gorgeous and unquestionably expensive. Marble is also porous and will absorb stains. Bakers appreciate its cool nature on an island or as a counter inset. Granite is stain resistant. Slate is emerging as a less expensive alternative for countertops. There are many different types of slate, but all are dramatic with their dark gray greenish hues. Vermont slate is more solid in color, whereas Brazilian slate—which I have just installed in my kitchen and adore—has a pattern of swirls in a dark sea of greeny gray. Slate counters should be sealed with a penetrating sealer and cleaned with warm water and gentle liquid detergent. They need a monthly coat of mineral oil to keep up their rich luster. Slate can chip, and like all stone countertops, they are hard and unforgiving when something drops on them.

**Concrete** Concrete is a handsome, long-lasting alternative for countertops and backsplashes. The seamless counter is either custom-built at a factory or built on site if it is too large to transport or if the counter runs around a sink or stovetop. Due to special additives, it is less susceptible to cracks and chips than the concrete used in sidewalks. It can be tinted or treated to resemble more expensive materials such as granite or slate. The surface is sanded, the edges are slightly rounded, and a protective sealant is applied. Properly prepared and installed, concrete won't crack or dent and is water resistant. These countertops are heavy, however, so be sure that a suitable frame support is installed to carry the weight.

Stainless Steel There's no fear of hot pots or spills damaging this tough material, although acidic liquids can discolor steel if left too long. Scratches and dents are expected, and over time they become part of the steel's patina. With a cool smooth surface that is perfect for bakers, stainless steel has an appealing commercial sleekness and mixes well with other materials, especially light woods. Clean with a mild detergent and then polish with a dry cloth. An occasional wipe-over with baby oil will get rid of smears and help keep the sheen.

Glass Glass makes a functional and attractive backsplash or countertop for contemporary-style kitchens. To make a durable backsplash, 3/8-inch-thick sheets are adhered to the wall with silicone and finished with corner bolts. Colored or opaque glass can be used as well as clear glass over a colored wall. Clear glass on a white wall will give a watery aqua tint. Tougher 3/4-inch glass must be used for countertops and heat-resistant glass must be used around the stove. Glass is growing in popularity. It's available in many colors, with clear, opaque, milky, and metallic finishes. Glass tiles are sold in mosaic or standard tile size. A glass tile surface tends to be uneven and so is better used as a backsplash.

## makeover opportunities

Because they are required to be such hardworking surfaces, countertops aren't as amenable to makeovers as cabinets. But if color is your problem, there are possibilities for the most common of all, plastic laminate counters. They can be painted. Turn to page 164 for complete instructions. And if a surface can be painted, you can choose any color and create any look you want. A textured technique such as faux granite or marble will hide any irregularities. It is a temporary solution, but with care, as long as you don't chop on it or drop on it, a sealed painted surface is a good solution.

Tile counters can be revived as well. Usually it is the grout that is stained, creating an eyesore. You can regrout and choose a colored grout as an accent. Seal the grout to help prevent future staining. Chipped or cracked tiles can be replaced without having to redo the entire surface. It may be impossible to match the color, so introduce another color or put down a small selection of decorative tiles, and the job will look professional. Painting over a tiled countertop is not recommended.

A backsplash can be a real work of art. There are many inexpensive and easy paint choices for this area and it's a perfect place to play with paint, as the area is so small. Try stamping on faux tiles with a kitchen sponge. The wall color should be the color of the grout. Leave a $\frac{1}{4}$-inch gap between the square stamps. Paint a row of metallic diamonds or you can even use paper to create a decoupaged pattern. As long as you seal the area with several layers of varnish, the backsplash will be durable. In the modern kitchen on page 91, I simply covered the backsplash area with three coats of high-gloss varnish to give the illusion of glass.

# sinks and faucets

Like all other product lines for the kitchen, sinks come in a wide variety of designs and materials. When choosing what's right for you, keep in mind how you use your kitchen. Are you preparing food and cleaning up for a large family? Do you love to entertain? If so, then you will want to have two or even three sinks, with one large enough to fit the roasting pan and pasta pot. On the other hand, if the microwave and coffee machine are your only concerns, then choose a sink with more flash than practicality.

The two most common material options, stainless steel and white enamel, have been broadened to include solid surface, soapstone, slate, and composites. For bar or preparation sinks, brass and copper can be included as well. However, these require a high degree of upkeep.

Design and installation details also vary. Self-rimming sinks have a lip that sits on top of the counter. Undercounter models sit below the countertop, showing off the edge of the counter material. There are sink designs that include a drain board, and others that are built extra deep or quite shallow. There are integral sinks, which are made of the same material as the countertop, usually solid surface such as Corian. One long mold includes the tops and the sink. In most models, the back rim has holes precut for the faucet and taps.

Brazilian slate is a stunning alternative to the traditional granite countertop.

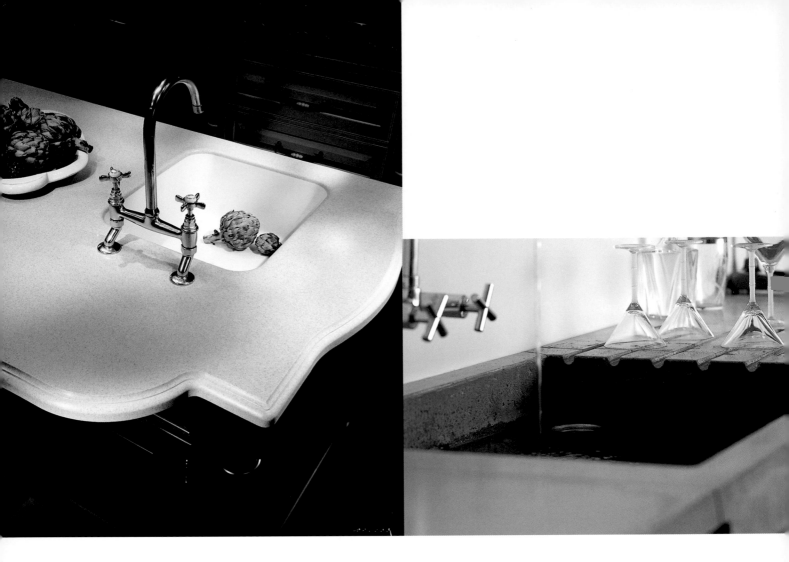

Again, there are many combinations and styles for faucets and taps. Your overall kitchen design as well as your preference for water control will help you to narrow down the choices, as will cost. Here is an overview of what is available. It's worthwhile visiting the Web as well as your local kitchen store to see all your options.

## what's available

**Stainless Steel Sinks** This is the most common material for sinks, and for good reason. It won't rust, is relatively gentle on china and glass, and is easy to clean. It can also withstand sudden temperature changes. Stainless steel is the most practical choice for any kitchen and comes in a full range of sizes and shapes. There is a noise factor, more so if there is a food disposal included, but an insulating coating applied to the underside of the sink will help.

CLOCKWISE FROM TOP LEFT: The golden tones and arched shape of these fixtures enhance the room's fine wood cabinetry.

The shallow concrete sink and countertop complement a kitchen that is more about style than practicality.

A deep farmhouse-style enamel sink is an efficient choice and a country classic.

A soapstone sink works equally well in a contemporary, country, or traditional kitchen.

Enamel-Coated Cast-Iron Sinks A good-quality enamel-coated cast-iron sink has a hard glossy finish that won't dent. It is resistant to scratches, stains, and chips and there is minimal noise vibration. Enamel is tougher on glassware than stainless steel. The apron front style is a classic country look that is now being included in designs that mix modern and old.

Acrylic and Fiberglass Sinks These composite materials are made to resemble the look of enameled cast iron, but the sink is considerably lighter. The color permeates the depth of the material, which hides nicks and scratches. These sinks are quieter than stainless steel and more stain resistant than enameled cast iron. Solid surface materials such as Corian come as a sleek, seamless counter that can include the sink and even carved out drainers. There is a stunning variety of colors.

Stone Sinks Soapstone and slate sinks are made from separate slabs of material; care must be taken to ensure that the edges where the slabs meet are properly sealed. The stone is durable but can chip. These sinks are very heavy and somewhat costly, but add an authentic element to a country kitchen.

Faucet Styles The faucet, made up of matching tap and levers or handles, is the most hardworking element in the kitchen, so it is imperative that you choose a style that suits your needs. There is a constantly expanding choice available today: Spouts alone can vary in height from a standard 6 inches to a soaring 20 inches. The type of arc made by the spout is not only a style point but will affect cleanup as well. Most faucets swivel to give you water access in more than one sink and the latest models have a pull-out spray spout. These are fabulous for cleaning out pots. A spray attachment can be adapted to the spout or installed separately at the back of the sink. Wall faucets are ideal if you are short on space in a small kitchen. In this case, the faucet handle is commonly a single lever or knob that allows you to control the temperature and pressure of the water at the same time.

**Faucet Materials** The simple polished-chrome tap has plenty of competition, and the finish can also be brushed or satin. For added visual interest, and cost, you can choose from brass, copper, nickel, and gold-plated faucets, as well as solid-color paint or enamel in white, ivory, and black.

## floors

The kitchen floor takes more abuse than any other interior surface. It withstands scuffs from constant foot traffic and spills that range from scalding hot soup to sticky sauces and toast crumbs. Daily sweeping and damp mopping with disinfectant detergents also take their toll. Flooring manufacturers are aware of these stresses, and offer an exciting choice of materials that are not only durable but also handsome and stylish.

## what's available

**Vinyl** This is the least expensive and most common floor product laid in kitchens today. It's available in tiles or rolls and comes in solid colors and assorted patterns, some that imitate the look of real stone and wood. Vinyl is functional and comfortable, waterproof, slip resistant, and easy to keep clean. Quality increases with thickness, but sharp objects will leave cuts in vinyl that cannot be repaired. This is a synthetic material that will melt or scorch with fire or heat. Some of the latest technology has managed to incorporate photo images into vinyl, with tiles of leaves, pebbles, and even water as interesting options.

Linoleum For decades, this was the standard for kitchen floors. Linoleum is soft and warm underfoot, yet extremely durable. It fell out of favor for a time, perhaps due to a lack of color and design choices, but this has all changed. Linoleum is back with a full range of designer shades. Made from natural ingredients, it is impervious to heat; colorants and patterns permeate the material so it ages well; and the product is inherently hygienic. Linoleum can be one solid color, it can be bordered, or patterns can be cut to create unique designs. If you do decide to purchase linoleum, be aware that there are some retailers that don't recognize the difference between linoleum and vinyl flooring. Make sure you get the right product. Linoleum is not much more expensive than vinyl but there is a world of difference in quality.

Linoleum also makes a good area mat. Lay pieces in front of the sink and stove to prolong the life of your existing floor or to make a softer resting place over ceramic and stone floors.

Prefinished Wood and Laminate Planks These planks are pre-cut, generally tongue and groove, and are made of a plywood core with thin strips of real wood or wood veneer on top. If the veneer is thick enough, you will be able to sand and refinish your floor at least three times. A tough top coat is applied at the factory, which adapts well to a high-traffic area. This type of floor is fast and easy to install, and can be laid over cement, plywood, or old wood floors. Floating floors (installed without nails) can be picked up and relaid in another area or home. Another option is a product that uses photographic images of real wood grain that are laminated to a fiberboard core for a most realistic-looking plank floor that is pre-sealed and ready to install.

Wood The beauty, warmth, and gentle give of a hardwood floor make it an inviting choice for the kitchen, especially since eat-in kitchens have gained such universal appeal. There are drawbacks, however; the protective varnish coating does wear and needs to be sanded and reapplied every five or six years. Also, with the natural expansion and contraction of the wood planks, dirt will get trapped in the cracks. Liquid spills should be mopped up quickly before they have a chance to penetrate the wood. Hardwoods are the most expensive. Choose from maple, walnut, oak, or the rarer cherry. Pine is a soft wood that is less expensive; it is ideal if you plan to paint the floor. If you are staining a wood floor, always test on a patch first. All types of woods take stain in a different way. Stain is permanent, so if you don't like the color, it must all be sanded off.

**Ceramic Tiles and Stone** Reminiscent of Mediterranean *piazzas* and Mexican *casas*, these hard-wearing materials bring a cool, earthy ambiance to any kitchen. This beauty comes at a price, however, as stone is tiring and cold underfoot. The finer stones such as slate, limestone, marble, and granite are costly, although there are also budget-friendly ceramic tiles sold off the shelf in matte and gloss finishes. Remember that smooth stone may look sleek and gorgeous, but it is dangerously slippery. Grouting between the tiles gets dirty and stained, so plan to regrout every few years and use a dark grout.

**Cork** Traditionally laid as tiles, this environmentally friendly product is soft, warm, and quiet to walk on, but it will wear over time. It is absorbent in its natural state and should be carefully sealed. Greater durability and an interesting choice of colors have made cork enormously popular. The material is now available in planks; the cork is adhered to medium-density fiberboard; it is precolored or left natural and sealed. The planks are laid as a floating floor with no nails or glue required, and can be removed and reused in another space up to three times.

Rubber Rubber floors have always been a favorite with commercial architects and designers because of their great durability. Rubber flooring is now being sold for residential use as well and is available in many colors other than black and gunmetal gray. There are a variety of patterns from geometrics to imitations of slate. Rubber's textured surface is skid resistant, soft and warm underfoot, and easy to upkeep. It is usually available as large tiles that are easy to cut into patterns and borders. You must use the suggested adhesive to lay the rubber, and some floors require sealers or top coats for sheen and protection.

CLOCKWISE FROM TOP LEFT: it is hard to believe that these wide planks only resemble barnwood. This laminate flooring incorporates photo images of real wood.

A hot rolled steel floor is not for the faint of heart. Once laid, though, it's not only stylish and modern, but also warm in the winter and cool in the summer.

Cork floors are soft and warm underfoot, and they are now available in stylish colors and patterns.

Technology has brought vinyl into the twenty-first century. It's now available in an incredible variety of colors and designs and also incorporates photo images like the pebbles seen here.

Rubber is tough and long-lasting, easy to lay, and modern. It's ideal for lofts, condos, and apartments.

Metal The growing trend for industrial-style kitchens has led to steel floors being used outside commercial properties, especially in loft apartments. Steel can be purchased in sheets or as steel or aluminum tile. The most common finish is shiny silver steel, which is available with different treads. I recently laid a kitchen floor of hot rolled steel, a common construction product. The tiles are about 3 feet square with a bluish slatelike color. All metal floors must be laid over a completely flat plywood or concrete surface since any bumps will soon dent the material. If necessary, a new plywood floor should be laid. The metal plates or tiles are glued into place, each butted tight against the next. You cannot grout between metal tiles. Hot rolled steel is sealed in the factory but it needs a monthly wax to stop rusting. This is a high-maintenance floor, but it does give an edgy look to a family kitchen.

Concrete In the right environment concrete floors can add a cool contemporary flair. Builders are now offering home buyers the option of keeping the concrete floors they have just laid rather then covering them with wood, vinyl, or carpet. This gives the kitchen an industrial look that can be softened for comfort at work areas, such as in front of the sink or stove, with rubber or linoleum mats. The concrete can be painted or stained in a variety of patterns. A concrete floor is heavy and may not be an option for some houses.

## makeover opportunities

Kitchen floors, no matter what the material, do require upkeep. Ground-in dirt, stains, cuts, and chips can all result in a rather dingy display. If you are giving your kitchen a facelift, but would like to wait a few years before replacing the floor, there are some solutions that will offer a fresh, clean look at little cost.

Wood floors can be sanded down to remove dirt, stains, and worn sealers. Then you can restain or paint. Unless you are familiar with the sanding process, I advise using a professional for the job. Wood is soft and will gouge easily. Some wood veneers and patterned-wood laminates can only be resurfaced if cleaning and sanding them will not harm the old surface. These materials are difficult to repair and paint will not stick to a damaged surface.

If you are building a new home or renovating, you may wish to save up a little longer for that special kitchen floor. As an alternative, plywood and particleboard subfloors have their own charm if you add a coat of stain to them. You can block off geometric shapes with masking tape, apply a stencil pattern, or paint a solid color. Here's your chance to try out a color you wouldn't normally have the nerve to go for or to opt for the glossy white floors often found in beach properties.

Old linoleum and vinyl floors can also be painted. The exception is the cushioned-floor style that gives when you walk on it. The movement of the material makes it impossible to paint, as cracks will soon appear where you stand or walk. Because linoleum and vinyl floors are made to resist sticking, you must first prepare them properly. Wash the floor thoroughly with a heavy-duty cleanser such as trisodium phosphate (TSP), rinse, and dry. Then sand the surface to give it tooth, and finally apply a high-adhesive primer that is meant to cover shiny surfaces. Once the floor is properly prepared, you can apply any water-based paint or floor paint. Finish with three or four coats of varnish to seal and protect your work. Even in the most carefully applied jobs, paint on linoleum or vinyl will eventually chip, but this is a great short-term solution.

You can also use linoleum to fashion a floor mat to cover worn areas in your floor. Paint your design on the back of a piece of vinyl or linoleum. (It must be paper-backed.) These mats will sit flatter than their canvas floor cloth cousins. It's easy to cut any shape and size and the edges don't require hemming.

As with counters, chipped ceramic floor tiles can be lifted out and replaced and new grouting added to refresh the floor.

An old wood floor in a country kitchen was painted in a tartan design. The heritage colors match the milk paint cabinets, but I used latex paint and added four coats of varnish for protection.

# walls

With cabinetry and appliances taking up most of the kitchen, the wall area is usually limited. But this is no reason for the walls to be ignored in your design plan, especially as paint is the least expensive item in the whole kitchen. A splash of color will make the room come alive; even the use of unusual materials on the wall will create dimension and depth. A sheet of Plexiglas bolted over a luminous color (see page 99) or plywood stained to look like a wall of exotic teak (see page 90) are inexpensive ways to add interest.

Any surface in the kitchen should be scrubbable. Today's water-based paints are far more durable than those of the past, so there is no need to apply glossy oil paint. Many paint manufacturers make a latex paint designed for kitchens and bathrooms. It's advisable not to use a matte or flat paint on the walls. A satin or velvet finish is best if you don't want a shiny surface.

Chalkboard paint is a hard-wearing writing surface that is a practical friend in any kitchen. It could be applied to one whole wall, a panel, or even on the door. It's perfect for messages, recipes, phone numbers, or just to keep the little ones occupied.

Kitchen wallpaper is back in vogue but in very different styles from the patterns of the '70s and '80s. Modern designs include metal effects, oversized prints, and murals. Choose a product that has a protective coating. There are papers designed for kitchens and bathrooms that are better able to withstand heat and moisture. Textured papers are an ideal way to cover cracked or uneven walls.

Plaster There are types of plaster available that are far more sophisticated than the traditional stucco. But even stucco is seeing a comeback, less as a rough stippled effect and more as a softly textured surface rubbed over with lightly colored glazes reminiscent of Mediterranean or Mexican homes. Venetian plasters incorporate marble dust into the mix. This makes a durable, tough finish that can be sealed with varnish or waxed and buffed to a high sheen.

Bare plaster is also durable. It creates a matte, chalky surface with a light, subtle texture. I have used bare plaster on all my kitchen walls, and although it is porous, stains wipe off easily. If you want to paint bare plaster, it must first be sealed with primer or the paint will just be absorbed.

As a modern alternative to paint, a deep chestnut stain was wiped over the surface of this birch veneer wall. I let the stain build up in the grooves to give them definition. Please see Partition Wall on page 90 for instructions.

The quickest way to change the look in any room is to add color, even if there is little wall space with which to work. A bright splash of color or a delicate pastel will draw your eye away from a not quite perfect counter or dated appliances. A colorwashed fresco look will heighten a Mediterranean mood—see page 169 for colorwashing—whereas a metallic pearlized paint or a stenciled country border will create very different effects.

To ensure the finish will last, good preparation is crucial when you embark on painting your kitchen. Because oil paints were used in many older kitchens, you must remember to use a good-quality high-adhesive primer that is designed to go over an oil base coat before applying latex paint. There are also primers that will seal in stains like smoke or nicotine. The walls must always be washed first in TSP or white vinegar to remove all the grime and grease. See the Back for Basics chapter at the back of the book for instructions.

# lighting

You perform many different tasks in the kitchen, which is the central hub of the home. It's a place to prepare, cook, and eat meals as well as a favorite gathering spot for socializing, doing homework, watching television, and paying the bills. Too little light will cause eye strain and poor posture as you bend to make out what you are doing. If the light is coming from a single overhead source, you will be working in a shadow. The perfect combination of lights will relax you and allow you to use every area of the room to its best advantage. Before you embark on a lighting system, decide how and where you work in the room. Take note of the natural light and where it falls at each time of the day. How can you best enhance it? There are also many different types of surfaces in the kitchen: shiny ones will reflect the light; matte will absorb it. Since friends often end up in the kitchen at a party, you should have a way to turn down the lighting.

Ambient Light This is general or overall lighting, which fills the room and comes from either a single fixture or spotlights in the ceiling. If you have a window or a door in the kitchen, then sunlight will add greatly to this type of light during the day.

Task Lighting There is no room that demands more task lighting than the kitchen. Ambient light, since it comes from above, causes your body and upper cupboards to cast shadows on your work surface. Bright and efficient task lighting should therefore be installed under the cabinets and directed over an

Colorwashed walls in tones of yellow ocher complement and highlight the variety of surfaces: steel, wood, and marble.

island, stove, and table so that you have focused lighting on the job at hand. It is an important safety feature as well as being aesthetically pleasing.

Accent Lighting Small spotlights can be installed inside glass-front cabinets, over display shelves, and above the upper cabinets. These low-wattage lights will cast a soft glow on items you love to look at. They draw your attention to a special corner of the room or simply create a quiet mood. In an open-plan home you'll want to use accent lighting to keep a low light in the kitchen while the family occupies the living or dining area, rather than turning off lights in the kitchen and having a black space.

Dimmers It is a treat to be able to control the mood in the kitchen with the flick of a switch. Light dimmers will allow you to adjust the ambient and task lighting to suit your needs. While you are eating, turn down the lights over the sink and work counters, dim the overheads, and enjoy the atmosphere created by your accent lighting. When the dishes are cleared away, go back to full power overhead for the homework. This versatility is not only useful, but you will save on electricity and bulb replacement by using only the amount of light you require at any given time.

BELOW: There is nothing more precious in a kitchen than natural light.

OPPOSITE: Today's modern kitchen may not afford undercounter light, but task lighting can come from many sources.

# elements
## of the bathroom

The scope of products and designs for the modern bathroom is vast. Ask yourself how the room will function, because this is a room that can be custom-built around your most intimate needs. Are you working around a family, or is this a bachelor bath? Do you have a spare bathroom for guests? Is there someone with special needs in your home? What kind of space is available and can you extend it? The bathroom typically contains a bath, but does everyone in your family prefer showers? If so, then why install a bath, especially if space is limited? Many of the boutique hotels cropping up in major cities no longer have bathtubs, but instead have the latest in fancy showers. Bathroom countertops no longer need be standard height. In fact, with today's taller population, it is advisable to add a few extra inches for comfort.

The humble bathroom has undergone a major transformation over the last two decades. We now see spaces that range from basic and utilitarian to grand and sybaritic. Pampering ourselves has become a priority, and what better place is there to set aside a few private moments every day? Where possible, we are expanding bathrooms to accommodate our commitment to exercise and meditation. Whirlpool bathtubs are a common commodity and shower stalls can be designed with multiple sprayers and heat lamps. Bathroom fittings look more like furniture than cabinets. Bathrooms have grown so spacious compared to a century ago that we can fit in a chaise longue or armchair.

No matter how simply or lavishly outfitted, however, the bathroom must first be a clean, safe space. We are most vulnerable here, and require adequate room to maneuver around the toilet and sink, and to towel dry after bathing. This is the place for rounded edges and slip-free floors. Easy-care, water-resistant surfaces will last longer and make daily cleanups simple and quick.

With the wide range of bathroom fixtures available, there are styles to suit every home and budget. A bathroom can boast state-of-the-art mechanics and materials and look Victorian, art deco, or contemporary. Color, lighting, and accessories will play a significant role in creating your own retreat.

Although makeover opportunities are limited for toilets, sinks, and tubs, there are wonderfully creative ways to update the look of a bathroom by applying a fresh coat of paint or plaster to the walls, cabinetry, wall tile, and even some countertops. Adding a few eye-catching details can make a huge difference.

Cast-iron tubs are once again back in fashion, and the exteriors can be painted to fit your decor.

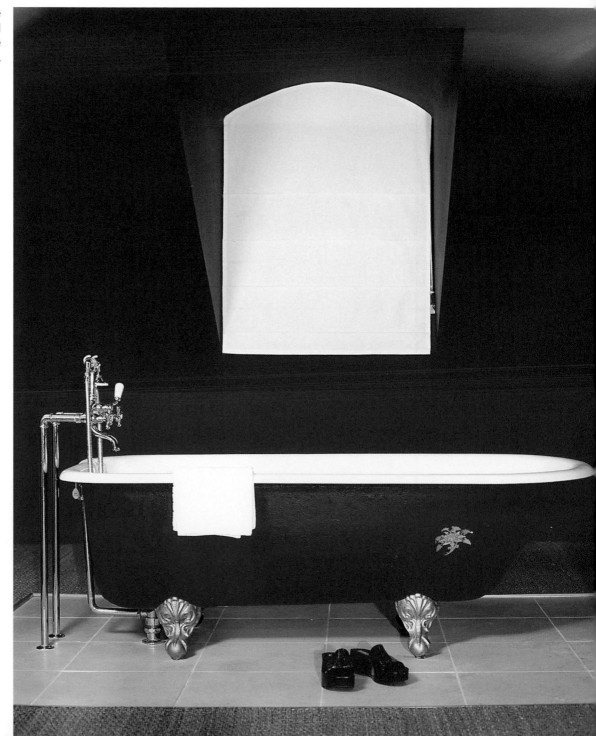

# bathtubs

Bathtubs come in sizes and shapes to suit every space, body, and style. If you consider soaking in the tub a luxury, then take the time to visit a showroom and sit or lie in different models. Length, depth, inner curves, faucet and plug placement, and, for whirlpools, nozzle angles should conform to your body.

The most common materials for making tubs today are acrylic and fiberglass. A thick acrylic coating over a fiberglass frame results in a nonporous, shiny surface that is warm, smooth, and easy to clean. Although acrylic is lightweight, it's a good idea, especially with the less expensive tubs, to add reinforcement to the frame to prevent creaking and eventual cracking from flexing. The most common color choice for tubs is white with the occasional ivory or cream. There are few other color choices available, unlike the avocado, brown, navy blue, and turquoise styles so popular in the '70s and '80s. We soon learned that colored tubs were impossible to keep clean since every soapsud and water droplet showed. White is the safest color and will complement every style of bathroom.

Although most baths are made from acrylic, enamel-coated cast-iron tubs are still being manufactured. Many people prefer the solid feel of this classic tub, whether it is an original or a reproduction. The older models could once be found at flea markets, and even dumps, but not anymore. Old cast-iron tubs are now quite valuable, especially the Victorian ones, which were built in a variety of shapes and sizes. Today, they can be found in restoration yards or at antique dealers and specialty showrooms that sell and restore antique claw-foot baths. Old or new cast-iron baths are very heavy and may not be suitable for many of today's newer homes. You will need a well-reinforced base to set the tub on and a strong team of helpers to muscle it into your bathroom. The enamel can chip if a heavy object is dropped on it.

On the high end of the scale there are bathtubs that cost as much as a small car. If your budget is unlimited, then so is the choice. Today's design icons are producing bathroom fixtures that are pieces of art. Philippe Starck's bathtub creations, like the Victorian claw foot, are freestanding. Oval shaped, they offer the practicality of an optional towel rod running under the thick rim. The fashion seems to be once again for freestanding baths, some of which have chrome legs and bars.

Bathtubs can be sunken or they can sit on platforms. They can be sculpted from steel to fit the body comfortably. Even copper tubs, once thought to ease arthritis and other ailments, are back. There truly is a bathtub for everyone.

If your bathtub is badly stained or chipped, it can be resurfaced by a professional, but this is expensive. There are also liners available for some bathtub models that slip over the old shell. However, it may be just about as cost effective to start fresh and buy a new tub.

If you would like to change the look without replacing the tub, you can build a bathtub surround. Wainscoting, wood panels, tiles over a plywood base —anything you could put on a bathroom wall would be appropriate, although wood will need to be sealed.

A standard acrylic bath has been dressed up by applying wood panels. Boxing in the bath and hanging an oversized shower curtain creates a theatrical bathing spot.

The exterior of an old claw-foot bathtub can be decorated with paint, stencils, stamps, and even metallic leaf. In fact, some new models come with the surface ready for paint. A good-quality primer and sealer will keep the surface protected for years. Please turn to page 128 for complete instructions on silvering this type of tub.

# showers

Nothing wakes you up faster in the morning than an exhilarating shower. In Asia they say that fast-running water enhances positive energy. I believe this is true; surely there can be no better way to start the day. The basic requirements for a shower are a sprayer connected to a water supply; a drain; and, in most cases, a curtain, wall, or door to contain the water. Traditionally, the most common arrangement for home bathrooms was with the shower as an integral part of the bathtub. With the fixtures attached down by the bath, you could sit or stand and spray yourself manually. Alternatively, plumbing was threaded up the wall, and a nozzle attached permanently for the hands-free shower. As showers became more popular, the bathtub was replaced by a simple floor with a lip high enough to keep the water contained.

Shower units take up less space than a full-sized bathtub and can be config-

The heads of rain showers come in different sizes; the bigger the head the bigger the shower.

ured to fit into corners and other awkward areas. These units come in a range of materials from acrylic to tile, glass, and stone. Fancier custom units can also be built from wood or concrete. The mechanics available include multi-directional nozzles and overhead sprayers that can be adjusted to settings from rain-shower soft to a pulsating massage. A small stool or bench will turn this space into a personal spa.

# sinks

Sinks are competing with the new sculptural bathtubs for design attention. Who would have thought the common bathroom sink could become a thing of beauty? There are sinks made of glass, hand-painted ceramic, steel, stone, and marble; sinks that sit like a piece of art on the counter; and sinks mounted on the wall. Sinks can stand as a pedestal or be set into a vanity unit. There are even ceramic sinks reminiscent of the time a bowl sat on a dresser long before the arrival of indoor plumbing. Sinks can be square, round, oval, or long and troughlike.

Think about how your bathroom sink is used. Is it simply for washups? Are there children in the home, or a man who shaves? Also take height into consideration, because you don't have to settle for the standard 32-inch to 34-inch-high sink if you are shorter or taller than average. If the bathroom is small, you may want to house the sink in a cabinet to conceal cleaning products, a shoe-shine box, extra toilet paper, and other bathroom paraphernalia.

Pedestal sinks stand alone with the plumbing pipes beautifully concealed. Half-pedestal sinks are mounted to the wall but have the pedestal to support the sink and hide the pipes. This design offers more foot space and takes up less floor space. There are sinks that appear to float out from the wall, with the plumbing concealed behind the wall. If you are installing a sink with a countertop or as an integral part of a cabinet unit, you may choose to under- or over-mount the sink or have it run flush with the counter.

Materials for making sinks must be solid, waterproof, and easy to clean. Vitreous china, porcelain, and acrylic are the most common, offering a glossy surface that's easy to disinfect and shine. For a striking custom look, laminated safety glass is available, and its natural aqua tint complements contemporary spaces. Stainless steel is lightweight and tough, and while used more in the kitchen, it brings a durable allure to the modern bath. Even plumbing is getting its day. Once hidden away behind walls and cabinets, the new wall sinks show off all their chrome pipes. Some of the most exciting plumbing can be found in the bathrooms of trendy restaurants, and these custom commercial designs are gradually infiltrating the home.

Stone is a natural material for both sinks and countertops.

Glass is a refreshing alternative for sinks.

# toilets

Toilet designs have been modified to efficiently use less water. To maintain a unified look, toilets, sinks, and bathtubs are available that match each other. Colors, including white, vary from one manufacturer to another, a point that may not be noticeable until fixtures are installed side by side in your bathroom. Like bathtubs, toilets are mostly sold in different tints of white rather than in the array of browns, blues and aquas of the '70s and '80s. Toilets with sleek lines and the tank hidden behind the wall are growing in popularity. You can choose a silent flush option—it's a little costly, but worth it. Steel, once restricted to industrial, army, and prison use, is now hip in the home. When you purchase a toilet, sit on it in the store. They vary in height and length. Make sure you plan for plenty of knee room where the toilet will be installed.

If your existing toilet is in good repair, but doesn't fit into your design scheme, it's possible to create a covering for the tank from wood or fabric and to replace the seat. Toilets cannot be painted.

# faucets and fixtures

The artistry and innovation in bath fixtures is a wonder to behold. Faucets arch high, bend sinuously, and twist gracefully in order to provide us with an instant flow of water. Chrome, stainless steel, nickel, copper, and brass are all available in matte, shiny, or brushed finishes. Traditionally bathroom faucets were found in pairs—a tap for the hot water and one for the cold water with a handle on top of each to turn the water on and off. Now there is usually one tap or faucet with the controls for water temperature and flow on either side or engineered as part of the faucet itself. New styles and expensive materials can come with a big price tag, but this is a perfect place to splurge. The plainest bathroom will take on a luxurious tone.

Today's modern toilets have their workings well hidden.

Taps, once purely functional, are now pieces of art.

# countertops and backsplashes

The countertop and backsplash that surround the bathroom sink should be as water-resistant and durable as possible. All seams, whether between sections of the counter or around the sink and fixtures, must be carefully sealed so that water can't leak through and cause damage.

Ceramic and glass mosaic tiles are heat- and water-resistant and come in an endless range of colors so you can create any design scenario you choose. Grout will collect dirt and stains and requires freshening with a grout pencil or regrouting every few years. The actual tiles can last indefinitely.

Solid surface materials such as Corian are custom molded for a seamless shape and are strong and durable. Laminate countertops are constructed by adhering a layer of acrylic or veneer over a plywood, particleboard, or medium-density-fiberboard base. These tops can scorch and stain and will dull over time. Never use an abrasive cleaner on them.

If you are unhappy with your plastic laminate countertop, and are working with a limited budget, it is possible to update the look with paint. Please see page 164 for step-by-step instructions for painting over plastic laminate. Even with a good sealing coat, paint will chip with constant wear or if something heavy drops on it. This is a fun but short-term solution.

Glass and stainless steel counters are contemporary alternatives that share water and stain-resistant qualities. Water drops are noticeable, so upkeep is constant.

Natural stone, porous marble, and slate have to be sealed against water and stains. Each has its own appeal, and although costly, they always add a luxurious touch.

# cabinets and storage

Bathrooms serve as action central in the morning when you have little time to wash and prepare for the day. Soap, creams, cosmetics, a hair dryer, curlers, razors, and myriad other accessories fight for space and need to be accessible and safely stored. Towels, mats, and bathrobes require an airy spot to hang dry. A well-thought-out storage plan is essential if you want an organized room.

It is easier to keep the counter clean and sanitary if bottles, brushes, and tubes can be either put away inside a cabinet or lined up on shelves. When room is tight, look for space in corners, or hang racks on the walls. If you have children or pets, cabinets should have doors to secure medicine, cleansers, or other health hazards.

I drew out the shape of the backsplash on a template
and had it cut from a slab of statuario marble.

Cabinets can be re-created with the help of a coat of paint to complement a new or refreshed bathroom style. In the terra-cotta bathroom shown on page 120, doors were removed from the built-in storage unit under the sinks and the surface and shelves were treated to a faux cedar paint effect. Small white fabric panels add to the spa atmosphere.

Bathroom cabinets are generally made of the same materials as those found in the kitchen and can be refaced following the same methods. Turn to the Back for Basics section for instructions on how to paint over wood and laminate.

The over-the-counter sink allows for plenty of storage in a small bathroom. Instant drama is achieved with the black-and-white color scheme.

Hooks are a space-saving option for hanging damp towels, and the multipurpose hotel-style rack is a handsome and practical storage solution as well.

A wall of built-in drawers and shelves is a luxury, offering plenty of space to store towels and extra toiletries in this large family bathroom.

# floors

Your choice of flooring will have a big impact on the bathroom environment. It will set the tone visually, but more important, the material will generate a tactile response. Ceramic and terra-cotta tiles are cool and hard underfoot. Marble and granite look and feel opulent, while wood is warm and rustic. Vinyl flooring is an inexpensive alternative that comes in colors and patterns that imitate more costly stones and tiles but it is not as durable; cuts and tears develop easily. Cork is a renewable resource that makes an excellent floor, although it must be sealed.

Rubber-backed bath mats will help to prevent accidents on slippery, wet stone surfaces. Linoleum and rubber are two materials that make durable, warm, nonskid floor coverings. They are available in colors and patterns from young and exuberant to straightlaced and traditional.

If your bathroom floor is in poor condition, then it should be replaced. Loose or broken tiles and torn or worn areas are dangerous and water damage can develop that is costly to repair. Periodically check the seals between the floor and fixtures and recaulk them when necessary.

## makeover opportunities

Wooden floors can be sanded and refinished with paint or stain. A good-quality plywood floor can be painted to imitate expensive materials such as granite or marble, or decorated with a whimsical design. (See the High Sierra Powder Room on page 138.) Always seal wood floors with three or four coats of varnish for durability and protection.

# walls

The walls in a bathroom are often a combination of different materials, with, for example, tile around the bathtub and behind the sink, and drywall elsewhere that is either painted or wallpapered. Even wall areas that don't get splashed have to withstand steamy heat, so the material must be at least moisture resistant.

There are paints that are formulated especially for bathrooms and have a mildew retardant in them. You can also add two layers of varnish for extra protection. But it is most important to apply paint to a thoroughly dry surface and then to allow time for each coat of paint to dry and cure properly. This will mean not using the bath or shower for a few days in order to ensure good adhesion.

LEFT: A black-and-white checkerboard design makes this tile floor versatile and sophisticated.

BELOW, RIGHT: An inexpensive alternative to real limestone is travertine marble cut in the opposite direction. Instead of seeing the veins, you see markings and color very similar to limestone. Here I laid 16-inch slabs with $1/2$-inch grout space.

BELOW, LEFT: Tumbled marble tiles are literally tumbled together in large drums to give the impression of timeworn stone. Here, a pattern in the grout line was left ungrouted and instead filled with pebbles. The different stones work well with the plaster wall.

RIGHT: This antique mosaic floor is all that remains of the original decor in a 1920's apartment bathroom.

Wood paneling in the form of wainscoting around the lower walls can be stained or painted and makes a timeless decorative detail for the room. Always seal the wood against moisture.

Concrete is appearing as an interesting contemporary alternative for bathroom walls. It can be tinted and applied rough or smooth. It must be allowed to dry for five or six days and then sealed.

Glass and glass block allow light to filter through and are an airy option for walls around a shower or between a toilet and sink.

## makeover opportunities

Bathrooms are the smallest rooms in the home. It is possible to design a fresh new look at very little cost and time with a few coats of paint. If you have outdated fixtures or are renting, don't be discouraged. Instead, draw the eye to an exciting new color or wall finish.

Stripes are always a hip, sleek option, painted in a bold contrast such as the deep blue and white horizontal stripes seen in the bathroom on page 124. Vertical stripes make walls appear higher, whereas horizontal stripes visually open up a small space.

Plaster applied to bathroom walls adds texture and mood. Layers of tinted plaster can be applied one on top of the other to build up a smooth fresco feeling. Concrete can also be tinted to stone or terra-cotta shades. This can be applied right over shiny tiled walls, although proper preparation is necessary (see page 157 for details).

Wall tiles can be painted as well. This is a good solution if the original color of the tiles is not to your liking. They must be thoroughly cleaned and then a high-adhesive primer applied in order for the paint to adhere. You will paint over the grout as well. The tile shape will not be camouflaged, but the color will. To cover up the tiles around the shower and bathtub wall, marine or melamine paint is most appropriate. Always apply varnish for added protection.

## lighting

Requirements for lighting are twofold in the bathroom. You will want a mirror and good task lighting over the sink and in or around the shower area, and an overhead fixture to light the room generally. If the room is small enough, it's possible to combine these two with wall sconces or spotlights. A dimmer switch is a necessity for your spa bathroom so that you can turn the lights down low, light the candles, and enjoy a relaxed soak in the tub.

This bathroom wall radiates with a mix of textures
and shades of blue from pastel to mauve.

# kitchen and bathroom makeovers

It is tremendously rewarding to give your kitchen or bathroom a facelift. Even a minor change such as a fresh new color rolled on the walls will have a major impact on your daily routine. These are expensive rooms to update, but don't let a minimal budget discourage you. Replace what you can and then revamp the elements that have to wait. The following makeovers prove that imagination (and the right surface primer) are worth their weight in gold. Your dream kitchen and spa bathroom are closer than you think.

This funky modern kitchen was designed on the tightest of budgets. Standard wood cabinets from a hardware store were painted in a milky tangerine. Plywood countertops were covered in stainless steel, and to make the room look larger, the backsplash was covered in a sheet of mirror. The floor is chocolate-colored cork; see page 37.

# retro reno

ORIGINALLY BUILT IN the mid-1980s, this kitchen was sterile and badly needed an update. Aaron, the homeowner, had begun the process by purchasing a few of the latest appliances—a new stainless steel refrigerator and a drawer-style dishwasher. But it was the white laminate cabinets that overpowered the space. The kitchen functioned well except for the small island that housed the cooktop. Aaron loves to cook and his dream was to have a larger central island with a new cooktop and all his pots and pans within easy reach. He had a healthy budget, but it did not stretch to a complete "gut and start from scratch" job. Our choice was to either change all the cabinets or spend the money on a new stove and cooktop. We all agreed that the latter was the ideal road to take. We were inspired by the vintage '80s linoleum floor. It was in excellent shape and its geometric pattern was back in vogue. For our palette, we combined retro shades of turquoise and blue with the latest in today's chrome and steel. The cabinet doors were painted turquoise with the occasional block of blue to break up the monotony of so many doors. The wooden handlebars were modernized with metallic paint and high-gloss varnish. (See page 148 for painting over laminate.) The big job was the island. First the old cooktop was removed along with the countertop. We kept the original base but applied mortar patch to the surface. This gave the impression of a solid concrete base that anchored the island in the center of the room. A new countertop was cut and then covered in stainless steel. For the backsplash, we added mirrored tile cut to fit directly over the existing tile. A potrack hangs over the island and shows off the stainless steel cookware, completing the effect of a hands-on kitchen.

*before*

## color conversation

Blue is usually a cool, soothing color but a greeny blue turquoise is lively and exhilarating. From blue to green, the range of colors is vast, from powdery robin's-egg blue at one end to pistachio at the other. Turquoise has gone in and out of vogue but it especially captures the spirit of the '50s and '60s. Paired with stainless steel and dashes of white, turquoise complements the clean lines of today's fitted kitchens.

# mirrored backsplash

A mirrored backsplash is an interesting alternative to traditional ceramic tile. Mirrored glass is timeless; it reflects color and the images around it. And best of all, it is easy and inexpensive to work with. If you have never cut glass, you will be amazed at how simple the process is. A glass cutter, available at craft stores, consists of a tiny wheel at the end of a long handle that will cut glass, not your fingers. Nonetheless, make sure you wear eye protection and heavy gloves when breaking the mirror as the edges are sharp. The tiles can be painted with glass paint and then baked in the oven to permanently set the color. The paint needs to be added carefully to avoid streaks. Here we painted only a few random tiles to emulate the color block pattern of the cabinets (see page 163 for cutting and painting glass). The tiles were adhered over the existing ceramic tile with tile adhesive.

# open storage unit

Storage and display often go hand in hand in a kitchen. I adore these open units for their uniform shape. They are usually available in white laminate and are backless, designed to sit against a wall. To dress up this one, we first nailed a sheet of primed Masonite to the back. Individual squares were then painted in retro '50s colors to complement the rest of the kitchen.

# steel and concrete island

Stainless steel and concrete work beautifully together. Here, there is a synergy between the clinical smoothness of the steel countertop and the rough texture of the concrete base, both clean and modern to look at. The old countertop was removed to make room for a larger work surface. We kept the base and refaced it with concrete and mortar patch (used to patch exterior stone and brick). The concrete was spread over the laminate surface with a spatula. After this had dried slightly, a damp sponge was used to texture the surface. A silver-gray paint mixed with setting compound was then rubbed on to highlight the textures. Once sealed, the concrete is very durable and looks like a solid concrete base without the weight (turn to page 166 for step-by-step instructions).

# loft life

IT WAS LOVE at first sight when Anita was shown this loft, and she bought it immediately. She was passionate about the open space, high ceilings, and original brick walls. Her only disappointment was the small, open "builders' kitchen" installed on a small budget with low-end fixtures and fittings. Anita had little money left for renovations, so paint was the answer to jazz up the kitchen. Color is a powerful decorating tool and here it positively transforms the entire loft space. Anita had started the job herself by painting the wall above the cabinets and the ceiling a golden yellow. She soon became overwhelmed and self-doubt set in. She was worried that the color she had chosen would clash with the old brickwork. By the time I came on the scene, she had given up on the job. I thought the yellow was fine, but alongside the brick wall, the white cabinets and the brown tile, it was not terribly exciting. The solution was to add some drama to the cabinets and tile. The standard white laminate cabinets and wooden handlebars were treated to a vivid green and the dull brown tiles were painted deep blue. With the complementing colors, the room immediately came alive. Anita was so thrilled with the kitchen that we decided to extend the bar/counter so friends can perch there while she cooks. We accessorized with a few stainless steel pieces and an oversized light fixture. A standard kitchen ceiling light was replaced by directional halogens strung across the workspace. The thrill of this kitchen can be enjoyed from all over the loft apartment. (Turn to page 148 for instructions on how to paint over laminate and page 157 for painting over tiles.)

*before*

## color conversation

Combining a mixture of colors in bands or blocks will give an updated modern appearance to a space, and playing with once forbidden groupings is positively inspiring! The rule "blue and green should not be seen without a color in between" is given a farewell note in this kitchen. The cupboards are painted a deep fern green and the tile backsplash is a true blue. They sit happily together, inducing a calm atmosphere with a touch of surprise.

# quebec cuisine

IT IS NOT UNCOMMON to live in a century-old home in North America, but one that is more than two hundred years old is rare. Cherie and Peter spent years restoring their heritage house in Quebec to its original character. It was built by a ship's captain in the early eighteenth century, when Montreal was a bustling port. Like many old homes, each generation left its mark on the decor. Drywall had been added to some of the walls and this was removed to reveal the local stone. Old linoleum, plywood, and carpet were pulled up and the wide-plank floors were lovingly restained and polished. New ceilings were opened to once again let the old beams shine. The most garish imprint left by one of the previous owners was a standard white laminate kitchen. The challenge was to build a kitchen that complemented the age of the house but also incorporated the new stainless steel stove and wall oven. Eighteenth-century kitchens of this period were known as keeping rooms, a place where people not only cooked and ate but also slept. They contained a mishmash of furnishings, light-years removed from the streamlined built-ins of today's commercial kitchens. Although the unfitted kitchen was born of necessity, this look is once again in demand for its comfortable and homey style. There are two ways to re-create the feeling of an early North American kitchen. A selection of individual furnishings, including armoires, cabinets, shelving, and even chests of drawers, can be assembled. The second option, which we chose for Cherie's kitchen, is to build a set of new wood cabinets that each have a slightly different design and shape. In either case, the furnishings should be painted, as was usually the case in the old kitchens. We removed the upper cabinets to open up the room and to reveal more of the stone wall. Open shelving

## color conversation

Authentic milk paint colors are the same today as they were in the eighteenth and early nineteenth centuries. Originally associated with Colonial interiors along the Eastern Seaboard of North America, milk paint was made by tinting buttermilk or skimmed milk with pigments taken from the surrounding countryside. Clays, plants, and berries produced intense colors with a powdery finish. They were applied directly onto the bare wood and dried to a subtle sheen. Today, specialist paint manufacturers have managed to match up the exact colors used in historic homes from Vermont to Virginia. Traditional milk paint is available in small bags of pigment, but the true vintage colors can also be bought as commercial latex paint.

*before*

was built to display a collection of vintage containers and dishes. The storage lost was replaced by adding a large armoire (not seen in photo) at the back of the kitchen to house the rest of Cherie's dishes. The counters below were kept, but the doors were replaced with new paneled wood ones. The center island that housed the sink also stayed, but the old laminate was removed and once again wood and molding added. An open counter replaces the original upper and lower cabinets. It divides the kitchen and dining areas, and wheels make it movable and practical. Cherry-wood countertops link the lower units together. By painting each piece in a different heritage color we designed a new, old kitchen. (Please turn to pages 150 and 155 for instructions on painting with milk paint and antiquing painted wood.)

# brick and black

SAM GAVE US carte blanche when we did over his kitchen—with one stipulation. The only color he hated was black! It was not pure cheekiness that prompted me to propose a black kitchen but the belief that black could be both dramatic and sexy. We began by adding height to the cupboards with lengths of wide stock molding. This was attached with nails and carpenter's glue to the top of the cabinets. The new detail immediately changed both the dimension and the character of the kitchen. We kept the old, exterior hinges and added stainless steel knobs and handles. After preparing the woodwork, the cupboards were first painted in the brightest of red, the color of ripe fruit. This is the base that gives the overlaying black, which could easily look dull and flat, a passionate glow (see page 152 for step-by-step instructions for painting these

cabinets). The same red was rubbed onto the walls, but first I applied an orange base coat. Straight from the can, pure red can be exhausting. The color needs to be broken up with some type of texture. Finally, I colorwashed ocher glaze over the surface, which simultaneously tones down the red and makes the walls come alive. Plaster molds of urns piled with fruit were treated in the exact same way as the walls. They were hooked in place along the backsplash to add even more pizzazz. The glaze added to the paint makes the backsplash water repellent and easy to wipe clean. Since the budget we had to work with just covered the cost of paint, it was paint that we used to

## color conversation

Black is not the most likely choice for kitchen cabinets, but mixed with the right combination of colors, it can be stunning. Black is commonly associated with contemporary design and it is also an important decorating detail. It's often used to accentuate a pleasing shape, such as an architectural feature in a room or in a piece of furniture. Alternatively, black can cause less interesting areas to disappear. For instance, the kickboards underneath kitchen cabinets are usually painted black, as they serve no visual purpose in the room. Red is also a color that many people avoid in a kitchen. Hot and passionate, red is an assertive and vigorous color. To work, red needs to be combined with colors of similar strength and intensity. Separately, both black and red would be difficult to live with, but together they arouse the senses.

*before*

renew the bland laminate countertop. Three different colors—brown, light gray, and black, were sponged onto a white base to give the illusion of expensive granite (see page 164 for step-by-step instructions). The final challenge was the white refrigerator; it no longer fit in with the sexy kitchen. What Sam really wanted was a brand new steel refrigerator, but he got the next best thing for only a couple of dollars. Contact paper with the look of brushed steel was cut to fit each panel and pressed into place. When Sam saw the finished kitchen he was not only happily surprised but he had also completely forgotten his dislike of black.

# country colors

HAVING TO WORK WITH what you've got can be challenging and even disheartening. But every space has potential—all you need is a little imagination. There is a well-known decorator's axiom: "Overstate the positive and diminish the negative." This is the mantra I called on when I first saw Randy's kitchen. His apartment sits in the middle of a busy city, but Randy was brought up in the country, and his tastes are more rural than urban. The positive features of his kitchen were limited to some fairly new appliances and a city view. There was no shortage of negative features: old painted cabinets, a faux marble laminate countertop, a dingy linoleum floor, and the strangest painted cardboard tile on the wall. But the biggest problem was lack of funds; only the bare minimum could be spent. Paint was the answer. We began by choosing a mossy green for both the upper walls and the cabinets. The cabinet surfaces were then given extra dimension by rubbing on a dark brown paint to highlight the panels and detail. Although Randy had envisioned removing the fake tile, I was dubious about the state of the wall underneath so we opted again for paint. Inexpensive louvered shutters were used to dress up the wall around the small window, improving the proportions of the window and the room. The shutters were aged with paint to add some rustic charm. Finally, a long mirrored window frame, a flea market find, was refinished with paint and used to hang utensils, a practical and decorative feature. All the newly painted elements in the kitchen draw the eye away from the more negative features like the floor and countertop, which are now barely noticed (see pages 150 and 152 for aging cabinets with paint).

## color conversation

Green and yellow are natural companions, always young and springlike. Green, the color of life, is restful to the eye, while yellow is freshly optimistic. Although too much yellow can be hard on the eye, splashes of it can be balanced with the cooler shades of green.

*before*

# window frame storage

Old window frames are often filled with mirror instead of glass in country decorating. I hung a long, slim storm window frame on its side not only to reflect the kitchen but also to use for hanging kitchen utensils. A coat of white paint was roughly applied, then a thin coat of brown was painted and rubbed off while still wet. This is a simple antiquing technique. Hooks were screwed in 5 inches apart along the top of the frame and the whole piece was hung securely onto the wall.

1

step 1   *(Shot 1)* Sand any loose or flaky paint from the old frame. Roughly brush on a coat of white paint and let dry. Apply a thin coat of brown paint over the frame and, while still wet, rub off the excess with a damp rag, leaving brown behind in the crevices and highlighting imperfections.

# painted cardboard wall tiles

Sheets of board tiles were commonly used in the '70s to cover uneven walls. Instead of removing them and possibly unearthing a multitude of sins, I decided to brighten them up. The tiles were 4 inches square, so after applying a white base coat, I enlarged the pattern by sticking ¼-inch low-tack painter's tape around sets of four. Alternate 8-inch squares were painted green. A yellow glaze was then painted over the whole surface, including the white squares. This yellow over green illuminates the green, giving a sunny translucent finish. The tape is removed, revealing white grout lines that also add brightness to the overall effect.

step 1   *(Shot 1)* Apply a white base coat to the cardboard tiles. Let dry for 4 hours. Then use ¼-inch painter's tape to mask off groups of four tiles. Paint alternate tiles green.

step 2   *(Shot 2)* Mix a yellow glaze, 1 part latex paint, 2 parts water--based glazing liquid. Apply the glaze over the entire surface with a rag or brush. Cover both white and green tiles. Let dry and remove the tape to reveal white grout lines.

1   2

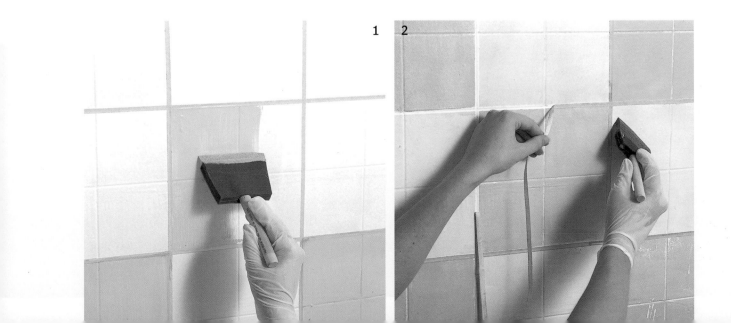

# cottage chic

FILLED WITH THE ENTHUSIASM that only a first-time homeowner can have, my friend Careen flung open her front door. My initial impression did not quite match her eagerness. Her newly purchased cabin sat overlooking a pristine lake, but the interior was dismal. It was also tiny, consisting of a long living area with a kitchen at one end. In addition there were two small bedrooms and a minuscule bathroom. The focal point of the cabin was the kitchen, so armed with sledgehammers and aided by several of her neighbors we ripped out the existing kitchen. Since the cabin had been built as a weekend home, everything was very basic, functional but frugal. By the end of the day all that was left were the guts of the cabinets on the back wall and the ones under the sink. We had also kept the fridge, the stove, and the sink. I wanted every element in the room to be white except for the walls and the floor. The first surface to tackle was the ceiling. There was no detail in the form of moldings or trim, so I added architectural interest by applying strips of $1 \times 4$-inch pine evenly spaced down the length of the ceiling and painted it all white. The cabinets were then reinvented by cutting out the middle of the doors and inserting glass. All were painted white. We found several pieces of secondhand furniture at the local flea market and painted them white. Careen had discovered an original old candy counter that had probably sat in the general store in town. Its glass top, which had once exhibited goodies, became a perfect display case for Careen's silver utensil collection. The floors are not real wood but planks of laminate flooring that have a photo image of rustic barnwood embedded in the surface. The expanse of white now needed a burst of color, so I chose for the walls an apple green that creates an atmosphere that is fresh yet soothing.

## color conversation

Choosing a color palette should be instinctive, emotional, and definitely personal. No other color raises the spirits quite like green. There are thousands of shades of green and each one creates a different effect. Green is the color of the landscape and represents balance and harmony. But it is this balance when combined with different colors that can change so dramatically. Green can be combined with just about any color, but in order to breathe, green needs lots of white. The impact is one of dynamic freshness.

*before*

# antiqued candy counter

Although it first felt like sacrilege to paint over the beautiful old oak of this piece, I stuck to my convictions and went for it. The whole surface was lightly sanded and then a high-adhesive primer was applied. This ensures that the base coat will stick to any stain or varnish and will also stop any wood resins from appearing through the paint at a later date. Once dry, I applied two coats of semigloss white paint, the same white used throughout the room. But, to make the counter look a little more important, a sienna glaze was rubbed over the surface.

### RECIPE FOR GLAZE

*1 cup water-based glazing liquid*

*2 tablespoons raw sienna artist's acrylic paint*

*2 teaspoons burnt umber artist's acrylic paint*

step 1  *(Shot 1)* Mix the ingredients, then apply the brown glaze with a brush over the dry white base coat, being sure to get into all the cracks and crevices.

step 2  *(Shot 2)* Wipe the glaze with a soft lintfree cloth, removing most of the glaze but leaving a small amount in the grooves to highlight the details.

1

2

# country cabinets

The first step in reinventing these wood-veneer cabinets was to remove all the doors. The interiors were given a fresh coat of white paint. We discovered that the doors each had an inset panel, so we used an X-Acto knife to cut through the veneer and popped out the centers. The frames were given the same antique treatment as the candy counter (see opposite page). Clear silicone caulking was squeezed along the ledge that had held the wood panel in place and glass inserts were pressed into position. Lace trim was glued to the shelves that show behind the glass-front doors. We removed the doors from one of the cupboards to offer an interesting break in the row of cabinets. The view is now fresh, open, and very country.

# breezy curtains

These white cotton sheers make a pretty picture at the cottage windows. I love unconventional and easy window treatments, and what could be simpler than clipping ready-made cotton panels over a row of upholstery studs hammered into the wood frame? The clips are available at hardware or office supply stores.

# laminate floor

Cottage life calls for no-fuss surfaces and that includes a floor that can withstand wet, muddy, and sandy feet. Wood is a natural choice, and original hardwood floors are a luxurious addition for country living, but beyond most budgets. I discovered a product that is a durable and affordable alternative. These planks have a photo image of real wood laminated onto their surfaces and are presealed. The planks click into place and can be laid directly over concrete or plywood with no nails required. (See photo on page 36.)

# rental redo

I OFTEN HEAR the words "I'm only renting, so there is no point doing any work in my place." Well, I strongly disagree. If you are renting a place for even a couple of years, it really is worth spending a weekend with a couple of friends to cheer it up. Brother and sister Petro and Christina are fellow students. Their rental was the typical small apartment with the usual pokey kitchen. It was also the official rental white. We are told that dark colors will make a room look smaller, but this is not necessarily true. A rich color palette can add so much drama to a room that size is irrelevant. I gathered together a group of Petro's friends and over two days we sanded, painted, and nailed. I have never heard so many "wows" as when Sunday evening rolled around and the kitchen was finished. The ceiling was left a flat white and a blue/mauve covered both the walls and the cabinets. This uniformity helps highlight the rugged beauty of the steel details such as the backsplash, cabinet handles, and shelving. We had lost storage space by removing the top cabinets, so we mounted steel shelves and hung chains in front of the window. Utensils hang from S-hooks. The window frame and the old countertops were painted in the liveliest russet and then sealed with one coat of glossy varnish. The blue, russet, and steel work happily together but they did need to be grounded. This was easily achieved by adding inexpensive linoleum tiles in the deepest charcoal. We had no budget for traditional kitchen lighting, so inexpensive clip lights were used. The hardest part of the kitchen facelift was persuading the landlord to give his stamp of approval!

*before*

## color conversation

Blue is chosen more than any other as people's favorite color. A solid blue kitchen, however, might be more than a little scary. But why not? Blue radiates energy, yet it can also be peaceful and comforting. It has the reputation of being cool, but mixed with the tiniest hint of red, blue moves toward a wonderful warm mauve. Blue mixes well not only with the reds, oranges, and yellows that are on the opposite side of the spectrum, but also with the greens and grays that sit on either side of it. Deep rust makes blue spring to life while the silvery gray tones of steel add some punch.

# corrugated tin backsplash

A little time spent wandering around a lumber or hardware store will reveal a world of fascinating materials. Textures, finishes, and materials that were originally designed for construction, plumbing, or electrical systems can be cheaply incorporated into your home as unique design elements. Here, corrugated galvanized metal panels were used as the backsplash. They were cut to size in the store and the edges were sanded down by us. You must wear heavy-duty gloves when you handle the panels with their extremely sharp edges. Once sanded and cut, each panel was held in place with cement screws and blue washers. Because the metal is galvanized, it will not rust.

# cabinets and hardware

The cabinets had been sloppily painted so all the lumps and drips had to be sanded down. The old paint was also oil-based and since I wanted to use latex, I first applied a coat of high-adhesive primer, which would grip both the original oil-based paint and the new latex base coat (see page 155 for details). This bluish mauve color is in close relation to the silvery patina of the hardware. Knobs were attached to the lower cupboards, but cleats, generally used for wrapping window blind cords, add an industrial touch to the drawers.

# storage strategy

Lack of storage is the most common complaint in a tiny kitchen. We had already lost one set of upper cabinets, which reduced Petro's meager storage even more. We did not actually remove the cabinet, just the doors, then tilted the unit on its side to give him open shelving. Storing pots and pans should also be part of the look of the kitchen. The view from the window is unexciting, so we used the space wisely and decoratively for hanging utensils. Large cup hooks were screwed into the top of the window frame and then lengths of chain were hung 6 inches apart across the space. S-hooks were used to hang a variety of kitchen aids.

# simple modern

DESIGNING A KITCHEN in an open loft is very different from the traditional home setup. In a loft the kitchen area is an integral part of the entire space. Since it is visible from the other living areas, every aspect of the kitchen needs to be part of the overall design. I wanted to keep the kitchen free of clutter and at the same time keep cabinets and furniture to a minimum. Andreas's bachelor lifestyle did not require rows of cabinetry for storing dry food supplies, crockery, and pots and pans. His domestic requirements were few—a work surface to mix his delicious martinis and a microwave to heat up his midnight snacks. A stove, refrigerator, and dishwasher were already there. We tore down the existing cabinets, and I designed a wall of lower cabinets with only floating shelves for easy access to plates and display items. These were all bought ready to install, but we refinished the flat-fronted cabinet doors with deep charcoal paint. We splurged on modern wall-mounted taps and on concrete countertops that were custom-made to fit the lower cabinet's base. This color choice of tones of gray is enlivened with steel appliances and chrome and lemon yellow chairs. The dropped ceiling was highlighted with a touch of the palest silver green. Warmth is brought into the kitchen with the application of wood veneer to a free-standing wall that was put up to hide the refrigerator from views outside the kitchen space.

*before*

## color conversation

Designers commonly use a tone-on-tone palette for a sleek, uncluttered space. Here charcoal-painted cabinets live comfortably with the silvery concrete countertops and walls of the palest gray. Colors that range from dark to light are monochromatic and soothing, but they do require unexpected splashes of color for warmth.

Lofts often have freestanding partition walls that can be dressed up as interesting structural elements in an otherwise undifferentiated space. We created an accent wall of wood that added texture and a warm, honey glow to Andreas's loft. We achieved the same effect as a wall of solid wood panels with a less expensive alternative—wood veneer. These are thin layers of wood that are glued to a plywood or drywall base. Veneers are available in most types of wood and can be stained in the same way. Here we applied a sheet of birch veneer to plywood cut to size, but before adhering it to the wall, we grooved it with horizontal lines using a router to give the impression of panels. The lumber store can do this for you. Once in place the pale birch veneer was wiped with a dark chestnut stain in smooth, even strokes in the direction of the grain. The stain was applied heavily in the grooves to make them stand out. Once dry, the entire wall was sealed with two coats of low-sheen varnish.

# concrete countertop

Stone, in the form of granite and slate, has for some time been used for countertops, but the popularity of concrete is growing. Do not be fooled into thinking that this material is less expensive than stone, though. It has become a favorite of many architects for its versatility in color, texture, and shape. In its liquid form concrete can be pretinted a variety of colors, and once poured it will assume the shape and texture of the mold. It can even have the same tactile quality as polished stone. In this kitchen, we had the sink, the draining board, and the countertops made as one uniform piece. The concrete was precolored a natural silvery gray. Once installed onto the top of the cabinets, it was protected with concrete sealer.

## varnished backsplash

Not all kitchens are used for large-scale food preparation. The design for Andreas's kitchen was conceived to complement the overall loft space. While practicality was kept in mind, this sleek design did not require a traditional backsplash. Instead I applied three coats of high-sheen clear varnish in a wide band above the concrete countertop. This protects the wall from splashes, it is easy to wipe down, and it suits the uncluttered tone of the space.

# marvelous
# mosaic

YVONNE LIVES IN AN OLD HOUSE in the city, but she had always dreamed of a country kitchen. Moving was out of the question and her budget was tight, with just enough for paint and a few small extras. Yvonne's two daughters, on the other hand, wanted a fun, lively kitchen that could show off their artistic talents. A compromise was achieved. The cabinets, although old, were in fine shape, so they were given two fresh coats of a delicate primrose yellow and new stainless steel handles (see page 152 for instructions on painting over previously painted cabinets). To bring in a country theme, we attached sheets of faux brick paneling to the walls and rolled on white paint thickened with plaster. Now it was the girls' turn. We spent a lovely afternoon drawing kitchen items and patterns. These were enlarged and

traced onto sheets of Masonite that were cut to fit the backsplash space. We then cut up black, white, and mirrored glass tiles to "color" in the drawings. The tiles were glued in place, leaving a thin space around each piece for the grout. A backsplash needs to be durable and one of the sturdiest materials is tile, either ceramic or glass. This surface was now easy to keep clean and designed in an innovative way to show off the children's artwork. We finished off the country theme by building a homemade pot rack. Lengths of plumbing pipe were joined together to make a hanging rectangle around an open wire rack.

## color conversation

Mellow yellow combined with textured white creates a sunny, bright kitchen that is not overpowering. Yellow in a kitchen is always uplifting, but it can also be tiring if it is too vivid or used too lavishly. Black and white will offer a natural balance. Daylight brings out the variations in color and texture between the roughly painted brick wall and the glossy smoothness of the mosaic.

before

# mosaic backsplash

Children love to display their artwork at home and here is a way of making it permanent. We used irregular pieces of black, white, and mirrored glass to create a pattern over the area of the backsplash. It is hard work to glue the pieces directly on the wall, so a sheet of Masonite was cut to fit snugly around the counters. The children's drawings were copied onto the board and the images outlined and filled in with the tiles. A small gap was left around each tile for the grout.

Glue the tiled board in place before grouting the design. (This will take a few pairs of hands to achieve.) Any holes for sockets should be cut before tiling. Once the board is in place apply tile grout over the entire area. Leave to dry and then wipe the surface with a damp sponge. Sweeping strokes will remove the powdery residue from the tile surface, leaving grout between the tiles.

# faux brick wall

To add a country look we turned plain walls into ones of painted brick. Sheets of faux brick paneling were cut to size and then nailed to the wall. A coat of primer was applied to seal the surface. White paint was thickened with coarse wall-texturing powder, leaving some of the lumps intact. A heavy pile roller was used to daub the surface to give the impression of old whitewashed brick walls.

step 1   *(Shot 1)* Cut the brick paneling to size and attach it to the walls with screws. Prime with a high-adhesive primer.

step 2   *(Shot 2)* In a container, mix 1 gallon of white latex paint with approximately 16 ounces of texture powder. Leave it a bit lumpy.

step 3   *(Shot 3)* Roll the paint mixture onto the walls, making sure to get in between the bricks.

# space within a space

OPEN-PLAN LOFT SPACES are favored for their airy expanses, but it is also this luxury that can cause big problems. The only rooms in a loft that offer any privacy are the bathroom and usually the bedroom. Kitchens, on the other hand, are usually seen from every angle. If you live in a loft, your kitchen must be part of the overall decor. Chantal's loft was funky and hip, but her small utilitarian kitchen was as basic as they come. So was her budget. Chantal was renting her loft apartment and did not intend to invest much money considering she would be there for only a couple of years. The challenge was to modernize the kitchen with an invigorating mix of steel and color. Stainless steel, although the most popular kitchen material today, is expensive. The solution was to paint the flat-fronted plastic laminate cabinets with paint that looked like metal. Hammerite is a type of silver paint that gives the illusion of a slightly battered metal. The walls were painted with the most exciting shade of acid yellow, a strong color if left alone, but we had other plans. We took sheets of corrugated plastic and cut them to fit the space around the cupboards, the backsplash, and an adjoining wall. The plastic sheets were held in place with large screws, grommets, and washers. As a functional divider between the living area and the kitchen, the island was an important feature. Because it was rather small, we replaced the top with a larger one and added large industrial wheels so the island could be moved around for a party. We finished off the space with dark gray rubber tiles on the floor, which help give the impression that the kitchen is a separate space in this open-plan loft.

## color conversation

Citrus yellow and silver are a stunning mix of hot and cool. A yellow this vivid alone on the walls would be exhausting to live with, but its heat is diffused with a covering of corrugated plastic. The bright yellow now flirts with the translucent quality of the plastic.

*before*

# metallic cabinets

Flat-fronted laminate cabinets are the ideal surface for a sleek, modern makeover. Hammerite is an exciting product to work with. It's available through paint and hardware stores. Once thoroughly cured, it is tough and durable. It can be applied with a roller, but take the time to practice on a spare board to get the feel of the application. Hammerite is also available in spray cans. Spraying can work well when painting intricate or hard-to-reach areas such as around table legs, but it's always advisable to limit spray use. Another note of caution: Hammerite should not be used on food-preparation surfaces. If you can't find this product, there are numerous other metallic paints on the market, but they must be finished with several coats of varnish for protection (see page 148 for instruction on painting over plastic laminate).

# rubber floor

Rubber floors have been a practical staple for hospitals, warehouses, and industrial spaces for many years. They are not only long-wearing and easy to clean, but also slip resistant. Now that the range of available colors and designs has become extensive, the home market is beginning to enjoy rubber as an alternative choice for kitchen floors. The existing concrete floor in this loft was an ideal subsurface, because the rubber tiles need to be glued to a flat smooth surface.

# yellow plastic walls

I love this idea. I had seen corrugated plastic used in funky offices over wild colors, but never in a home. Chantal's loft afforded me the perfect opportunity to try it out. The kitchen space was small and bland and begging for a shot of color. Citrus yellow is so vibrant it could overpower the whole loft space. What we needed was balance. This was achieved by diffusing the yellow with the corrugated plastic and painting the cabinets metal gray. The plastic is available in 4 × 8-foot sheets from hardware or building stores and can be cut easily to size with a jigsaw. Once the walls are painted, let them dry for at least 24 hours to allow any moisture from the paint to evaporate. Measure the area to be covered and then cut the plastic to size. To add to the industrial style the pieces of plastic were held in place with large screws, grommets, and washers. If the plastic is going around a backsplash, seal the edges with silicone.

# cheap and cheerful

DARK OAK KITCHENS usually work only in large rooms; in small kitchens they can evoke a real sense of heaviness and claustrophobia in an already undersized space. This minute galley kitchen is only 10 feet wide, and even if the owner had had the budget for a full remodeling job, there was no room to reorganize the layout. Instead the original wood cupboards were painted with a low-luster robin's-egg blue and new chrome handles were added (see pages 152 and 155 for painting cabinets). I chose a low-luster sandy beige for the walls and the ceiling. The reason for continuing the wall color onto the ceiling instead of leaving it the standard white was because the room was so

small: Color uniformity prevents the space from becoming too choppy. The effect of combining the two pastels is both intimate and cheerful. The money saved on the cupboards was spent on new white appliances and a rubber floor that gives the illusion of expensive slate. The biggest cost saver was the backsplash. Basic white glossy tiles were added above the counter, but instead of using the more common white grout I chose turquoise, not only to match the color of the cupboards but also to make an ordinary element look a little more special.

*before*

## color conversation

Robin's-egg blue is not quite blue yet it's not really green. It radiates the peaceful qualities of a still sea. But these milky aqua tones can result in very different impressions depending on the colors with which they are combined. Bright white will add freshness, while splashes of orange or red create an exotic contrast. When mixed with other subtle pastels and neutrals, there is no gentler effect. Calm yet compelling, subtle pastels always sit happily side by side.

# new shaker

THE NINETEENTH-CENTURY American Shakers lived by the creed "Hands to work and hearts to God." Their faith dictated that they should have cleanliness and order in both their daily lives and in their homes. These attributes made them famous for many things, notably their finely crafted furniture. Their designs are marked by clean lines and a practicality that makes them fit well with today's busy lifestyles. Shaker-inspired kitchens are now readily available from kitchen showrooms, but if you have the standard white laminate cabinets and drawers, you can easily convert them as a less costly option. In this ordinary builders' kitchen we re-created the Shaker look with paint and the special effect of trompe l'oeil. All you need is paint and an L-shaped stencil to add the illusion of paneled cabinet doors. One of the most innovative Shaker designs still used today is the peg rail, which would be hung around the room at varying heights. We added our own by nailing straight wood molding around the room and attaching the famous shaker pegs. Another storage solution was the plate rack, which also kept clutter to an orderly minimum. Using these elements, a Shaker-style kitchen will provide an efficient working environment as well as a tranquil and calm space.

*before*

## color conversation

The purity of Shaker houses was reflected in smoothly plastered white walls, but color was often allowed to finish the interior woodwork. Sage and olive greens, Colonial reds, blues, grays, and even black were created from pigments taken from the surrounding countryside. Today's Shaker-style kitchens afford the clean lines and practicality of the originals, but there is no reason why the colors cannot be a brighter version of their vintage cousins. Here, blue cabinets cool down hot yellow walls. Both colors complement the warmth of the pine floors and furnishings.

# trompe l'oeil panels on doors and drawers

We applied a dusty pale blue paint to the upper cabinets and the drawers. A deeper blue was used for the lower cabinets. Light detail was added with paint to create the illusion of inverted panels. This is incredibly simple and really does fool the eye. Two matching L-shaped stencils were cut out of Mylar. Two colors are needed for the illusion, one a lighter shade than the base coat, the other slightly darker. First check the direction of your natural light source. If the light is coming from the right, the top and left side of the panel will be painted in a lighter shade than the bottom and right side. Stencil the light bands (the highlights) on each cabinet door, which will give them time to dry, then apply the shadow bands. The effect is as simple and clean as Shaker style. Please see page 148 for painting over plastic laminate cabinets.

step 1   Cut an L-shaped stencil from a sheet of Mylar. Ours is ½ inch wide. Cut the ends at a 45-degree angle so that the painted panel strips will look mitered.

step 2   Apply two coats of the medium blue base coat to the drawers and let the paint dry for 4 hours. Place the stencil for the top and left shadow bands onto the drawer. Use spray adhesive and press firmly along the edges so that paint won't seep under the stencil. Using a small roller with just a bit of light blue paint, fill in the bands. Remove the stencil and repeat on the next drawer until they are all painted.

step 3   Position the second stencil so that now the cut-out bands are at the bottom and right. Fill them in with dark blue paint.

# shaker peg rail

This design, as practical and decorative today as when it was invented two hundred years ago, consists of a wooden peg rail running around the room that allows items to be hung and displayed. Wooden pegs are inserted into a length of 1 × 4-inch wood at regular intervals and painted the same color as the rest of the woodwork in the room.

# shaker plate rack

This simple, functional design is a popular space saver not only for country kitchens but also in contemporary rooms, where it may be constructed with plastic or metal. The original plate rack was built with pine boards and dowels. Holes are drilled 1½ inches apart and the dowels are glued into place. Two sections were completed at different heights to hold large and small plates; cup hooks line the bottom; and open shelves hold other crockery. The wooden rack is then stained or painted to complement the cabinets.

# tasty combination

THE TYPICAL COUNTRY KITCHEN can often look dull and stale. Wood cabinets, which are the hallmark of the rustic kitchen, are meant to be pleasant and homey, but I truly believe that you can have just too much wood. When my friend Jan asked me to help give her kitchen a facelift, my first impression was to either replace the cabinets or paint them. Jan loved her wood but she had far too much of it in this house. The kitchen alone had wood floors, cabinets, moldings, and trim. After a session of arm wrestling, a compromise was reached. We would leave the floor alone but she would allow me to paint the moldings and reinvent the cabinets. This turned out to be very suc-

cessful since not only did we produce a completely new look but we also managed to gain more storage. Panels were cut out of the upper cabinet doors and replaced with a lightly frosted glass. The dense orange of the pine was lightened up by "washing" the surface with a pale gray glaze. The lower cabinets were left intact but were darkened in the same way with a dark brown glaze. New steel handles were added and boxes made of medium-density fiberboard were built to sit on top of the cabinets. These provide useful display space, but note that I removed all the dreaded baskets of dusty dried flowers. The backsplash tile was rusty red, a color that was too similar to the pine cabinets. All the different elements should be broken up or they become one large mass in the room. I replaced the backsplash tile with a sheet of embossed tin, painted and

## color conversation

People may think that I have some kind of aversion to wood as I am always painting it. Not true, I insist, but I do find that too much wood can be dreary. Instead of having the regular upper and lower cabinets identical, give them separate personalities. Try painting them different colors. The top cabinet should be lighter than the bottom, or they will look top heavy. Or try glass cabinets above and solid below. Stain is also a great alternative to paint if the original cabinets are solid wood. Once again try different tones on the top and bottom.

*before*

rubbed for authenticity. The countertops are Corian, adding a modern sleek touch. The flowery wallpaper was removed and the walls were painted in a saffron yellow. Today's best kitchens, even country ones, have mixed features that work together. Here the wood and tin keep the kitchen classic country, but the Corian countertops and the openness of the cabinets bring us into the new century.

# glazed cabinets

The original pine cabinets were solid and in good shape. The doors were all removed and a jigsaw was used to cut out the panel in the upper doors. These panels were replaced with frosted glass, but first the wood was sanded down to remove any existing varnish. Glazes were applied to the doors with a kitchen sponge—a pale gray glaze for the uppers and a dark brown for the lower doors. This colorwash is always applied in the direction of the wood in a smooth, one-stroke action. The idea is to keep the translucency of the paint, which allows for the natural grain of the wood to peek through (see page 169 for step-by-step instructions).

# tin backsplash

Patterned tin was often used on ceilings and walls in the mid to late nineteenth century. The embossed tin sheets were not only decorative but also practical. They would last forever with the occasional fresh coat of paint added. Tin sheets are once again a popular and interesting decorating choice. There are plenty of patterns available in a variety of sizes. Here, the tin was cut to fit the area between the upper cabinets and the countertop. Steel cutters should be used and thick gloves are a necessity. Sand the edges as a safety measure. The tin needs to be primed to avoid any rusting—some panels come preprimed. A base coat of cream-colored latex was applied and then an ocher glaze was rubbed over the surface to highlight the pattern.

step 1  *(Shot 1)* Apply an alkyd primer over the tin panels with a roller and let them dry overnight.

step 2  *(Shot 2)* Roll on one base coat of off-white latex paint. Let dry. Mix an ocher glaze: 1 cup water-based glazing liquid, ¼ cup ocher latex paint. Apply the glaze with a paintbrush, then dab with a cotton rag, leaving the glaze behind in the grooves to highlight the pattern. Let it dry overnight.

step 3  *(Shot 3)* Apply two coats of acrylic satin-finish varnish.

# french twist

THIS IS ONE of the most incredible bathroom facelifts we have ever done. No new fixtures were bought, but the room has been completely transformed. It was an ordinary bathroom in a suburban home comprised of tiled walls and floor and a laminate vanity. The overall room was beige and dull. It did have one endearing feature and that was a coffered ceiling. I decided to enhance it with an ornate pattern. I think ceilings are important in a bathroom where lots of time can be spent lounging in the tub. The challenge was to transform all the existing 4-inch tile into slabs of rustic limestone. This was successfully achieved by applying pretinted stucco to the walls (see page 158) and pretinted concrete over the floor and the side of the bath (see page 160). We applied the

concrete to cover the grout lines and then, before it dried, we added a bigger grout pattern to create the effect of large pieces of stone. The clean line between the rich golden yellow around the bathtub and paler yellow on the walls is typical of the wall colors seen in homes in Provence. The same golden yellow was applied to the vanity, but first a high-adhesive primer was applied to the laminate surface to make sure that the paint would stick (see page 148 for painting over plastic laminate). I removed the blinds from the window and replaced them with shutters, a charming characteristic of so many French houses.

before

## color conversation

The sun-drenched colors of Provence are drawn directly from the surrounding countryside. Lively and warm, these shades encompass the creamy hues of raw plaster, pink, and orange. Provence's golden yellows combine with just about any other color but work best when applied with some form of texture. Straight from the can, commercial paint colors can be harsh and even dull. Mix "true" colors from artist's acrylics into a glaze and see how beautiful these are when rubbed over surfaces.

# painted ceiling

A coffered ceiling is one that is stepped up a little higher than the overall ceiling. It is purely decorative. The rest of the bathroom was designed to have the simplicity of a Provencal farmhouse, so a little opulence on the ceiling made a pleasing visual touch. Before I began the decorative painting on the ceiling, I applied a coat of regular white latex paint with a satin sheen over the ceiling paint. If a mistake was made, it would have been hard to wipe it off flat ceiling paint.

step 1    *(Shot 1)* Apply one coat of off-white satin latex paint to the ceiling and let it dry overnight. Using low-tack painter's tape, tape off an 18-inch border around the ceiling. Inside the band, loosely color-wash with a thin pale green glaze (4 parts glazing liquid to 1 part paint). Roll on the glaze and then dab it with a scrunched-up piece of cheesecloth to get rid of any roller marks and create a bit of texture. Remove the tape and let the paint dry.

step 2    *(Shot 2)* With a measuring tape and a pencil, mark out where each stamp design will be positioned on the ceiling. Ours are approximately 10 inches apart. We used half of the diamond design around the border edges, taping off the other half. Apply a thin coat of gold paint to the stamp with a 1-inch paintbrush, being careful not to get paint into the grooves. Too much paint will leave globs on the ceiling and blur the lines. Dab the stamp on a paper towel to remove any excess if necessary.

step 3    *(Shot 3)* Press the stamp firmly and evenly into position on the ceiling. Press uniformly over the entire stamp to have a clear imprint.

step 4    *(Shot 4)* With white paint and a stencil brush, stencil a simple border around the edge of the green band to add an extra highlight.

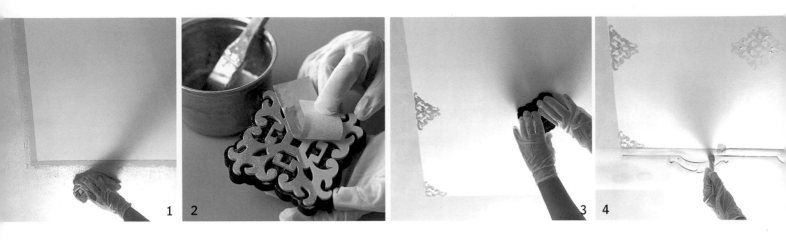

1  2  3  4

# decorative concrete floor

Limestone flagstones are used throughout Europe on kitchen and hall floors. They are deliciously cool on bare feet in the scorching summer months. Limestone also has the most superb tones of gentle color ranging from creamy whites to the richest honey. Alas, limestone in North America is extremely expensive but today's versatile plasters and concrete can replicate the real thing. Here, we used a specialized concrete. The tile surface must first be roughed up with etching cream to give it some tooth. We tinted the concrete the color of limestone and troweled the concrete over the grout lines to bring them up even with the tile surface. You will require as many coats as needed to cover the pattern of the tiles. Once you have a smooth surface, the last coat is marked out into large slabs before it dries completely. The edge of a spatula or a knife can be used. The shape and size of the slabs can be any size, irregular, or uneven. The whole area must be sealed with a low-sheen varnish for protection. See Resources.

Note: Check instructions on the concrete product. Some products come with etching cream or you can use a high-adhesive primer.

# style and simplicity

NABIL IS MY very talented editor on the TV series *The Painted House.* Inspired by the show, he had spent many a weekend doing up his own apartment. The final frontier was the bathroom. Tiny, and with no natural light, it was gruesome. The metallic wallpaper overpowered the small space and the vanity had seen better days. Looking on the bright side, the fixtures, sink, bath, and toilet were fine, standard white. Our first job was to remove the shiny paper. Metallic papers can be difficult to steam or soak off because of their durable finish. A good tip is to score the paper with the side of a spatula, being careful not to gouge the wall underneath. Soak the surface in warm soapy water several times, and the paper should then come off easily. We applied white paint to the ceiling to brighten up the room and to visually lift the low ceiling. Different textures of white—the smooth white porcelain sink, fluffy white towels, and matte frames—were also used to accent the room. The pinkish taupé applied to the walls complements the deep brown of the vanity, but it is

the high-gloss varnish on the mustard yellow countertop that gives this color scheme life. Each surface was treated differently. The ceiling is flat but the walls have a satin finish for better durability. The cabinet doors were first coated with high-adhesive primer, then two coats of latex semigloss brown paint were applied. One coat of midsheen varnish was added for extra protection. We made new drawers that double as a shelf under the large mirror. These were treated in the same way as the cabinets but painted the lighter wall color. The countertop gets the most wear and tear, so two coats of high-gloss varnish were applied over the paint to add extra luster and to ensure that they last as long as the original laminate tops. The dusky color scheme, enriched with touches of pure white and reflected by different sheens, gives this bathroom its modern edge. (Please see pages 148 and 164 for painting over plastic laminate and painting cabinets.)

## color conversation

A color scheme of dark peat brown, golden ocher and taupe is surprisingly seductive in a bathroom. These colors are masculine and earthy, yet together their properties are unexpectedly sensuous in such a small space. However, white is the important element that allows the room to breathe freely, drawing attention to the shapes of the fixtures and fittings.

*before*

# south seas bathing

IT WAS THE CLIENT'S large Indonesian-style mirror that dictated the colors for this bathroom. I wanted to create the feeling of exuberance that comes when you look out of a plane window onto the waters surrounding a Caribbean island—the color of the water as it meets a white sandy beach. That perfect shade when blue and green are mixed. Aqua paint was diluted with glaze and rubbed with a smooth rag over a white base coat. An aqua colorwash gives the illusion of floating beneath the sea. The delicate effect of the wall finish was balanced by the heaviness of the ornate frame. This old claw-foot bathtub was in pristine condition but I decided to do the reverse and make the outside look as if it had been washed up on a desert island, eroded and covered in rust. The burnt oranges, browns, and blacks and even touches of silver found in real rust are quite beautiful. By using all these paint colors, a realistic rust effect is easily emulated. The room was accessorized with the homeowner's shell collection and other memories of tropical beach holidays. (For colorwashed walls see page 169.)

## color conversation

Aqua is the most popular bathroom color, and for good reason. It is stimulating enough to wake up tired eyes in the morning but soothing as you prepare for bed at night. Aquamarine is where blue meets green; depending on the mix there are many different shades, ranging from turquoise to jade. Although white works well with aqua, the pair can look clinical, so a third color should always be added. Try a dash of black for a sharp contrast or tones of cream for '50s nostalgia. In this bathroom aqua was partnered successfully with different shades of brown and white.

*before*

# faux rust bathtub

It is not hard to find a piece of rusty metal. Study the different colors of the patina where the metal has begun to erode and I think you will be quite surprised at its charm. Keep this visual reference handy as you choose the colors for your faux rust finish.

*Note:* When using spray paints and spray adhesives, always wear a mask and work in a well-ventilated area.

step 1   *(Shot 1)* Prime the exterior of the bath-tub with a high-adhesive primer and let it dry overnight. Spray stencil adhesive thickly in random spots over the surface. This lumpy, uneven finish will make the subsequent coat of rust and black look as if real rust is forming naturally on the side. Let the adhesive dry for 15 minutes.

step 2   *(Shot 2)* With a splayed old paintbrush, loosely splatter rust-colored latex paint all over the surface to create a dense texture. While the paint is still wet, use a sea sponge to break it up.

step 3   *(Shot 3)* Spray black acrylic paint loosely and randomly to cover any white spots and create "stains" that seem to be coming out of the "rust."

step 4   *(Shot 4)* Using a second sea sponge, create clouds in random patches with a mix of silver and white paint. This should be subtle and gently applied. Go back over with a bit of rust and black if necessary, always softening.

*Note:*   The decorative, rust-like paint effect was applied over the whole outside surface, including the feet. Never paint the inside of a bathtub.

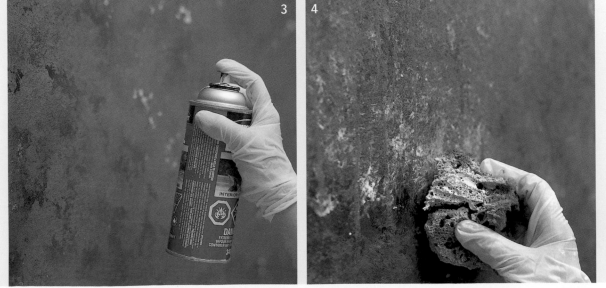

# terra-cotta triumph

THERE IS NOTHING more luxurious than a large bathroom; one that you can actually walk around in is a treat. This master bathroom was completely white on white—too sterile to be adjacent to the cozy bedroom. We kept the Jacuzzi, sink, and toilet and transformed the white ceiling, the white vanity, and the white tiles. See photo on page 145. The metallic white blinds were replaced with painted wooden shutters. The big job was covering all the wall tiles with a special stucco that is designed to go over tile. In order for the stucco to adhere, the shiny tiles needed to be etched or have a coat of high-adhesive primer applied to them. This stucco was pretinted a deep terra-cotta to

replicate both the texture and color of Mexican tiles. Alone it looked too flat, so the surface was color washed with a slightly darker tint to create the different tones found in this tile. Once dry, the entire surface was coated with a low-luster varnish for protection. This is adequate for the walls, but the stucco was not strong enough to go over the steps around the bath. Here we troweled tinted concrete over the primer. The concrete sets to a hard finish that will withstand water and climbing in and out of the tub. We removed the vanity doors and painted the ceiling and the vanity to look like the cedar planks found in a Norwegian sauna. I left the mirror in place but dressed it up by adding a frame. This was finished with a coppered patina that really makes the wall come alive. The only new purchases were stylish taps for the bath, two sinks, and a set of painted shutters.

## color conversation

A decorating scheme that uses strong colors will always make a big impression. Used as pure primaries these solid colors can be brash, but blended with a tint of another color they immediately become more sophisticated. Orange tinged with a little burnt umber translates to a glowing deep terra-cotta. Although bold, terra-cotta also has a softness and warmth that makes it easy to live with. There are a variety of shades of terra-cotta ranging from pale pinkish red to orangy mustards. They mix well with most colors but often require a contrasting color like a cool blue just to calm them down.

*before*

# terra-cotta tile walls

There are several ways to camouflage outdated ceramic wall tile. A new durable stucco allows tile to have either the rough texture of unglazed tiles or a smoother surface like limestone. Here we kept the shape of the existing tiles but wanted to add both the texture and color of terra-cotta tiles. It is imperative that the tiles are washed down well with TSP and then coated with a high-adhesive primer or etching cream. Either will ensure that the plaster sticks permanently to the surface. Once the effect is complete, the wall should be given two coats of varnish for extra protection (for step-by-step instructions, please see page 158).

## shutters

Plastic blinds are practical as they offer privacy, but they are not very decorative. A more stylish option is shutters. They can be bought in a variety of sizes from lumber stores. All you need to do is paint them and attach them with hinges and screws to the inside of the window frames. This alternative to traditional blinds allows for privacy but also lets light filter through the slats in ever-changing patterns.

# coppered mirror frame

The existing wall mirror was plain, so I dressed it up by gluing a 4-inch-wide wood frame to each edge. The lumber was painted with a patinated copper finish before being attached. You can buy these patina kits from art and craft stores. The kits have two solutions; the first is a metallic base, which is applied with a paintbrush, and the second is then dabbed on with a kitchen sponge. This second liquid reacts to the metal fibers in the copper coating and the patina gradually appears. The more solution you apply, the heavier the patina. Once you achieve a satisfactory effect, apply a couple of coats of midsheen varnish for protection.

step 1   *(Shot 1)* Prime the wood and apply two coats of rusty brown latex paint. Let it dry for 4 hours.

step 2   *(Shot 2)* Apply one coat of the base coat in the copper kit. Let it dry for 1 hour and then reapply.

step 3   *(Shot 3)* While the second coat is still wet, dip a slightly damp cellulose sponge into the second solution and dab over the surface. As it dries it will react with the copper and turn green. It takes approximately 1 hour.

step 4   Apply two coats of midsheen varnish for protection.

# true blue

STYLE DOES NOT need to be sacrificed to space. It is quite remarkable how the clever use of color and pattern can visually enlarge a room. This bathroom in a 1940s apartment building is no more than 5 × 10 feet. Nearly every detail from the walls to the fixtures was white. The common advice for making a room look as large as possible is to stick to white, but this does not always hold true. Stripes are a decorating trick that can drastically change the style and the shape of a space. Vertical stripes on a wall will draw the eye upward, giving the impression that a ceiling is higher than it really is. Wide horizontal stripes wrapping around a room will keep the eye moving, which will open up and widen the space. This effect was achieved beautifully in this small bathroom, even though I chose a strong, dark color. I left everything white except the area above the wall tile. There, a chalk line was used to map out straight lines 8 inches apart. Each alternate stripe was painted with two coats of ultramarine. Blue and white is a timeless combination. Think of the classic white shirt and blue jeans, the white stucco buildings and the blue sea of the Greek islands, and the everyday use of blue and white in tableware. In even the smallest bathroom, blue and white make an utterly harmonious pair (see page 168 for instructions on painting stripes).

*before*

## color conversation

Ultramarine includes the tiniest touch of red. It's not purple by any means, just a rich vibrant blue. This intense color has a fascinating history. Originally obtained in the twelfth century by crushing the semiprecious stone lapis lazuli, it was so expensive that it was used only for painting pictures. By the mid-1900s the Europeans were manufacturing an artificial ultramarine and the color become hugely popular for house painting. Blue in all its tones always works perfectly with white.

# en-suite romance

THIS BATHROOM sits at one end of a guest suite in an older home. Since the bath is in full view, it is the focal point of the whole space. Old cast-iron tubs have an evocative shape, gently curved and perched on their solid claw feet. I decided to make this bath even more sensuous by applying squares of silver leaf to the exterior of the tub and the feet. The remaining space was plain, so by adding a length of wainscoting to the built-in under the sink, a few new floating shelves, and the soft- est cornflower blue to the brickwork, the bath area became an integral part of the suite. The finishing touches were simple accessories such as a flea market mirror painted flat white, lots of fluffy white towels, a chandelier over the bath, and shimmering sheers for privacy. What more could a guest want?

## color conversation

Metallic details have been used for generations to add opulence to interiors. Although there are plenty of different types of metallic paints available, professionals prefer the more subtle effects created with metallic leaf. This may not be the most obvious choice for a bathroom, but why not? Gold or silver are synonymous with glamour. You will always find reflective sur- faces in a bathroom, with its chrome fittings, mirrors, and, of course, water. Silver will reflect the glow of the available light, casting a shimmering warmth in the room.

before

# silver-leafed bathtub

The outside of old cast-iron bathtubs is not always smooth: You may find dents and marks produced by age. I rather like these imperfections; they make a historical tub stand out from its modern acrylic copies. However, I toned down this bath's imperfections with the application of silver-leaf squares. The exterior of the bath was first cleaned with TSP and then a coat of high-adhesive primer was added. One coat of cornflower blue paint was rolled on; tiny bits of this base coat will peek through the edges of the silver squares. I used a piece of cardboard the same size as the sil-

ver leaf (this usually comes in the packet of silver leaf) to map out a grid with a pencil. A layer of aquasize, a special adhesive for leafing, was brushed over the whole surface. It is preferable to work in areas of six or eight squares at a time, or the size will dry before you get to it. Each sheet should go on in one piece, filling a penciled square. If part of the leaf doesn't adhere, add a little more aquasize to the bare spot and apply another piece of leaf. Once the entire surface is finished, three coats of varnish must be applied for protection.

step 1     *(Shot 1)* Prime the side of the cast-iron tub with an oil-based primer and let it dry overnight. Apply two coats of pale blue latex paint, letting the first coat dry before applying the second. Using a template the same size as a sheet of silver leaf, draw out the squares on the side of the tub with a pencil. This will help you to place the leaf.

step 2     *(Shot 2)* Apply a coat of aquasize with a foam brush. It goes on milky white. Let it dry to a tacky touch. It will go clear.

step 3     *(Shot 3)* To apply the leaf we made an applicator from a block of wood cut the same size as the leaf. A piece of velvet was glued onto one side of the block.

Each piece of leaf is picked up on the velvet side of the block and pressed onto one of the squares drawn on the tub. When the leaf is adhered, remove the block and press the leaf flat very gently with a soft brush. Let it dry for approximately 1 hour. Finish the whole surface and leave to dry completely. Spare bits of leaf can be used for the feet.

step 4     *(Shot 4)* Brush off any excess leaf with the soft brush. Apply water-based spray varnish to protect the leaf. Always wear a mask and work in a well-ventilated area when using a spray product.

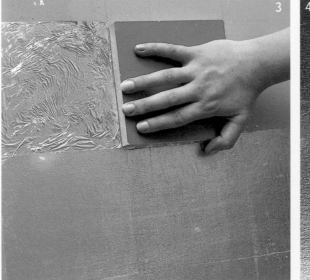

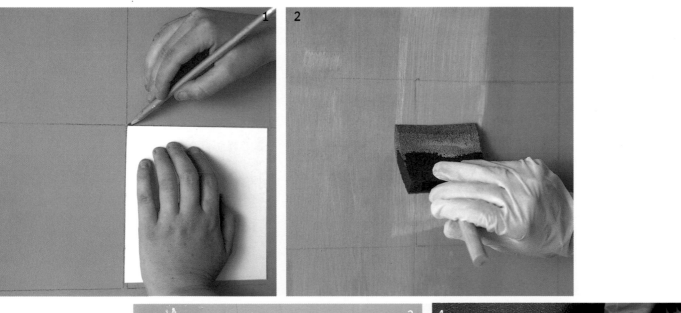

# tile style

THE COMPLICATED LIVES we lead today call for homes that are uncluttered and calm. I helped Andreas design the kitchen (Simple Modern, page 88) and bathroom in his new loft around the concept of a simplified living space. Apart from a few privacy walls, the large space was left open, with only the plumbing and electricals in place in the bathroom. Andreas is an unconventional character, and his vision of the ideal bathroom was very different from mine. He wanted a bath—but not one to lounge in. What he really wanted was a fabulous shower with a deep base. His ideas reminded me of some of the baths I have seen in Turkey, utilitarian but also beautiful, decorated with mosaic tile. The first job was to open up the drywall and add sheets of Durock around the bath area to avoid any water leakage. A shower base was molded out of concrete

and the inside of the base was covered with plain white tile. Building the concrete steps and the tub both required skill, so I advise using a professional who works in decorative concrete. Our budget was wearing thin by the time we came to choose the tile for the walls, especially since Andreas wanted walls of mosaic glass. These were expensive enough, but his preference ran to designer pearlized mosaic tile. At first he didn't believe me when I said I could replicate this high-end tile with concrete and paint. In the end, not only were the walls a success but we both loved creating the effect. The pearly tones and texture have an almost Zen-like effect when mixed with the cool steel fixtures and hardwood floor.

## color conversation

Celadon is a gray-green that varies in color from milky olive to foamy sea green. It can have a silvery hue rather like a willow or the underside of an olive leaf. Celadon was made most famous by the ancient Chinese when they used it as the glaze color for their porcelain and these pale smoky greens have been used for centuries to decorate interiors in North America and Europe. Over the last few decades it has been seen predominately in country decor, but its coolness now inspires many of today's more contemporary homes. Celadon lives happily beside pure white, but it also benefits from the occasional splash of a bright color or even colors similar in hue such as pale mauves.

*before*

# mosaic tile walls

stores. The grids are usually available in panels of about 3 × 4 feet. Start in one corner flush against the wall and mark the shape of the grid with a pencil. Use these as your reference of how much concrete to apply at one time. Concrete dries fast, so just apply from one to three grid shapes at a time, depending on how quickly you work. Apply the moist concrete with a trowel. It is very important that the surface is completely flat or the mosaics will be uneven. To ensure that the concrete is smooth, roll over the wet concrete with a damp foam roller. To create the mosaic shapes, press the grid into the wet concrete and remove. Repeat this around the room. If a smaller piece of grid is needed, it can easily be cut from one of the larger grids with a sharp knife. Once dry, the wall is painted with a primer. Use a deep-pile roller, making sure that the primer goes into the lines around the imprinted squares. Wipe over the surface gently with moss green paint on a flat kitchen sponge, leaving the white paint behind in the indented lines, replicating the effect of tile and grout. Next, a green iridescent gel is wiped over the tiles to give the illusion of the latest in shimmery mosaics. We even highlighted a few individual tiles with an artist's brush.

It is important to ensure that the wall area around a shower has been sealed with a building material like durarock so there will not be any water leaks. This faux mosaic tile effect looks terribly complicated, but in fact it is relatively easy. You will need self-bonding cement and one plastic checkered grid of the type that is used over neon lights in office buildings. These are available at lumber and hardware

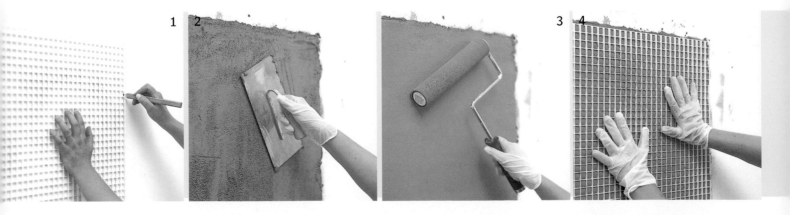

1  2  3  4

step 1  *(Shot 1)* Outline the plastic grid with a pencil on the wall. Mark off the whole wall.

step 2  *(Shot 2)* Trowel the premixed self-bonding cement about ¼ inch thick onto one grid section. (Once you have completed the process a few times, you will be able to work on two or three grid sections at a time.)

step 3  *(Shot 3)* With a slightly damp foam roller, go over the surface to smooth it out.

step 4  *(Shot 4)* You may want to wet the grid so it will not stick to the cement. Immediately press the grid into the wet cement and pull it off. Move to the next section and repeat the process (steps 2–4) until the wall is complete. Let it dry overnight.

step 5  *(Shot 5)* Roll on a coat of high-adhesive primer with a deep-pile roller to seal the wall and keep out moisture. Make sure the primer gets into all the indentations. Let it dry.

step 6  *(Shot 6)* Dip a flat sponge into moss green paint. Remove the excess, then wipe the sponge over the surface. The white primer will serve to create the effect of grout lines, so don't push the color in. Let it dry for 4 hours.

step 7  *(Shot 7)* Dip a flat sponge into iridescent green gel and make the same wiping motions as with the paint. This will add shimmer and life to the walls.

step 8  *(Shot 8).* Use metallic apple green and metallic emerald green stencil paints and accent some of the mosaic squares. Apply one coat of varnish with a deep pile roller.

THERE ARE SOME bathrooms that defy the best intentions of a paint makeover. This was one of them. Old and grungy, it needed a full facelift. As I have demonstrated throughout this book, yes, you can paint over wall tiles, even plaster over them, but the surface must be clean and free of mildew. This forlorn bathroom had seen many homeowners, so instead of trying to remove thirty years of grime we decided to start from scratch. We removed the tub, vanity, and partition wall and floor tile, keeping only the taps and the toilet. Today you will find everything you need for a bathroom renovation at your local building-supply store, including well-designed fixtures and fittings that are affordable. If you make the surroundings fabulous, inexpensive fixtures look great. We bought a new bath, sink, and showerhead and added a chrome rack. An inexpensive wood vanity was also bought and painted the same color as the walls. We added wood paneling around the lower walls, up around the shower, and even on the ceiling. Instead of using interior paint we applied exterior stain, which is extremely durable on wood in a steamy bathroom. On the walls above the paneling, Venetian plaster was troweled on in tones of cream and gold to match the pale yellow wood. The color palette of the walls is delicate so we grounded the room with a cork floor. The rich golden hues balance out the walls and the cork is warm and soft on bare feet. The window was a problem because although it was small and fairly high, it looked out onto another apartment building. Privacy was needed but so was any available natural light. The solution was etching liquid. We used the nonpermanent type, which cannot be removed with water but can be with methyl hydrate, so cleaning the window is fine. This was sprayed on over cut-out stars, which when removed, let the light dance through the clear shapes. No new plumbing was needed, so small and nasty was painlessly transformed into a sunny chic bathroom.

## color conversation

Undemanding and restful to the eye, pale yellow is an ideal choice for a small bathroom. These low-key yellows have less of the zing of citrus yellows or the warm glow of earthy ochers. Soft yellows do emit a sensuous beauty reminiscent of the most delicate sunlight on a spring day. Pale yellow ranges from creamy butter to the lightest primrose. A north-facing bathroom will always benefit from a shot of yellow while a sunny south-facing one can bask in its glory.

*before*

# cork floor

Cork is a common type of bathroom flooring in England, where it is warm and cozy on those far too frequently damp and chilly mornings. But cork is now becoming a popular choice in many North American homes. Once the homeowner is assured that cork is a durable and long-lasting alternative to linoleum or tile, it is a very interesting option. Many of the new cork floors do not need to be glued in place. A system of interlocking boards, already sealed, are cut to size and clicked into place. They can be removed at a later date if required and are easily washable. These specialty cork floors are becoming so popular that there is now a variety of colors available. Cork tile is less expensive but will not last quite as long as the interlocking type.

# wood and plaster walls

I added 3-inch-wide tongue-and-groove wood panels to the lower half of the walls, at the back of the shower, and on the ceiling to soften the hard lines of the bathroom. Molding strips cap off the top of the wood boards and silicone seals around the bathtub. The wood was finished with exterior latex stain. Any water-based stain designed for outdoor use is also extremely durable for wood in a bathroom and in a shower area. The upper walls were treated to the silky texture of Venetian plaster (please see page 170 for instructions on applying plaster).

# frosted window

This bathroom window was frosted with an imitation etching fluid. (Real etching solution will eat into the glass, which is not a good idea on a window.) This way the view is obscured but the window can still be cleaned with water or glass cleaner. If the frosting needs to be removed, a wipe-over with methyl hydrate will do the job. To add a decorative touch, stars were cut out of sticky-backed paper and stuck in a pattern on the window. After the etching solution was set, the stars were removed carefully. The sun creates fanciful patterns as it filters through the clear stars. Always wear a mask and work in a well-ventilated area when using a spray product.

step 1    *(Shot 1)* Clean and dry the window, ridding it of any streaks. Find a star design (we used a stencil) and transfer the image onto self-stick paper. We used dark blue self-stick paper. Cut out using an X-Acto knife or sharp scissors. Depending on the size of the window, you may need a few dozen stars.

step 2    *(Shot 2)* Peel the paper backing off the stars and stick them randomly over the window. Press down firmly so that the spray cannot seep under the edges. Spray the entire surface of the glass, holding the can about 6 inches away. Spray over the stars so that you will have sharp points when they are removed.

step 3    *(Shot 3)* Once the spray is dry, carefully peel off the stars, using an X-Acto knife to lift the edges. The stars will appear clear by day and medium to dark blue at night.

# high sierra powder room

THERE WAS A TIME, not very long ago, when bathroom fixtures were available in the strangest of color choices: Avocado green, harvest gold, chocolate brown, navy blue, and turquoise were some of the options. Today you would be hard-pressed to find many other than white. This narrowing of the choices actually represents a step forward, because your bathroom can be much more attractive designed around white fixtures than chocolate brown. Some of us, however, are stuck with remnants of these late '70s color and style trends. Lily's little powder room had shag carpeting on the floor; turquoise sink, toilet, countertop, and cabinets; and a wall of mirror above the vanity. All Lily wanted was a washroom that didn't make you cringe upon entering. There was no budget to replace the fixtures so the only choice was to have some fun. Inspired by the soft hazy hues of the Mexican desert, I decided to work with, not against, the turquoise. In fact, the turquoise worked admirably, evoking the semiprecious stones that are part of Mexican culture. The walls were given a sandy flat finish with Venetian plaster (see page 170). I love using this medium because texture and color can work happily together. The colors that peek through the sandy base were highlighted in a traditional Indian pattern around the mirrors. We first removed the large wall mirror and had it cut into smaller 14-inch-square pieces. These were glued back on the wall (make sure the edges are sanded smooth after cutting) and the pattern stenciled around them. I left the vanity alone, but painted the laminate cabinet doors a deep tan and added some new wrought-iron handles (see page 148 for painting over laminate). It was the floor where we had the most fun. The shag carpet was removed, leaving a plywood base. Here ceramic tile, vinyl, cork, or even rubber could have been used, but instead I opted to paint the floor. Living in a northern climate, I am always fascinated by the lizards and geckos that dart around brazenly in hotter countries. A huge stenciled gecko became the focal point in this powder room, living happily with his bronze cousin on the wall.

## color conversation

As the world gets smaller, our color boundaries expand. Palettes from every corner of the globe can be assimilated into our homes. Think of all the hues found in the world's different forests or the kaleidoscope of colors in the ocean, the shimmering shades of the desert or the powerful whites of the arctic. Even countries have their own color traditions, whether these be the delicate misty grays and blues of Scandinavia, the earthy tones of Africa, the delicious ice cream colors of the Caribbean, or the eclectic, vibrant mix found on every street in Mexico.

# painted floor

You will often find that wall-to-wall carpet sits directly on plywood. If the plywood is in good condition—meaning there are no areas that have rotted or are spongy from water infiltration—then it can be painted. After cleaning the whole surface and removing any nails, sand and fill holes. Then prime the floor with a good-quality primer. I chose a base coat of burnt orange, a color slightly brighter than real terra-cotta but a little less strong than pure orange. Once the floor was dry, the gecko was stenciled onto it. The oversized design would make one stencil too difficult to manage, so we cut him into several sections. First draw out the shape in the exact size onto a piece of craft paper. Lay Mylar over the top and transfer the design with a marker onto the plastic. The head and forelegs became one stencil, several stencils for the bulk of the body, then the back legs, and finally the tail. There is a $1/4$-inch gap between the pieces, which reveals the base coat. The gecko was painted with a roller in golden yellow. We outlined the shape by hand with turquoise. The floor was given three coats of semigloss varnish for sheen and protection.

# japanese gem

A BLACK BATHROOM might not be anyone's first choice but it is definitely a dramatic one. I loved the look of horror when I first suggested it to Scott but I can be very persuasive, so black it was. I was inspired by the lacquered *bento* boxes commonly used in Japanese restaurants. Their reflective and glossy surfaces play with the light, evoking a sense of Asian mystique. The green tiles and fixtures in this 1930s rental apartment bathroom were difficult to work with, and the white walls only drew attention to all the green. I applied black paint to the walls in a semigloss finish to allow the light to bounce back off its surface. I also painted the grout black with a 2-inch brush and then easily wiped off the residue from the tile. The black grout broke up the monotony of the green, once again adding drama. A black shower curtain was hung with steel grommets and oversized hooks onto a shiny steel rail. Bright red is the most common accent color in traditional Japanese design, so to offset the black we painted a huge red circle on the black ceiling. The red warms up the room and adds vigor as its reflection bounces off the walls. Corner shelves were made in staggered sizes to be practical and decorative.

*before*

## color conversation

Theoretically black is not a color but a tone of which there are many degrees, including soft gray-blacks, reddish blacks, deep browns, and sultry blue-blacks. These dark tones have names like ebony, jet black, anthracite, and eggplant. Whichever tone of black is used, the results will definitely be dramatic, especially when applied to walls. If used skillfully, black will create an intimate and sexy atmosphere. What is important when working with a lot of black is the sheen, because the color absorbs the light. If the surface is matte, black will appear dense, but when light hits a glossy black surface, the effect is vibrant. Black's main use in decor is to exaggerate other colors, making them come alive.

# shower curtain

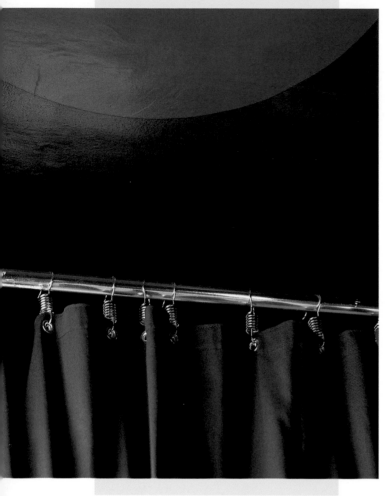

If you are not able to find a shower curtain to match or complement your bathroom's decor, they aren't difficult to make. We found black curtain panels and added grommets along the top edge. Grommets come in a kit that includes a tool for locking them into place.

step 1     *(Shot 1)* Measure and mark a small *X* across the top of the material every 6 inches, ½ inch down from the top. Cut a hole the size of the grommet opening over the *X* marks with sharp scissors or an X--Acto knife.

step 2     *(Shot 2 and Shot 3)* Work on a solid surface as you will be hammering. Lock the grommets in place using the grommet punch and a hammer.

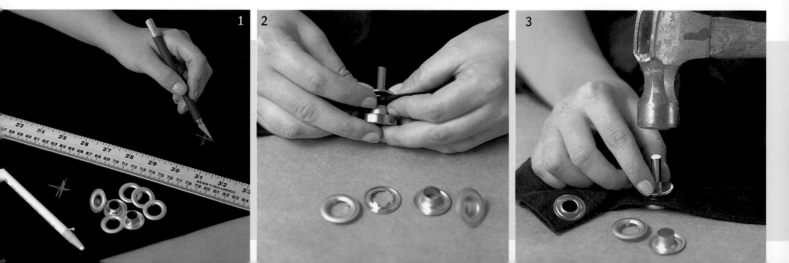

# corner shelving

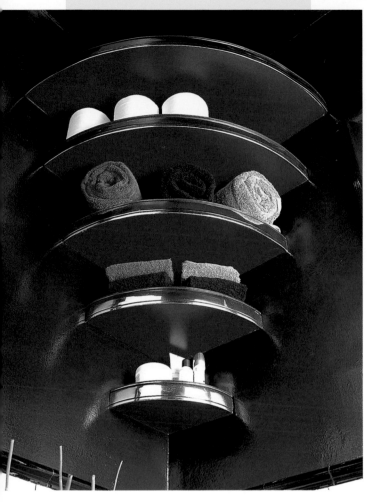

This shelving is a clever idea for small bathrooms where there is little room for any storage. The shelves sit above the toilet, but the last thing I wanted was for Scott to crack his head when he stood up. Neither did I want the shelves too high. One solution was to use graduated sizes of floating corner shelving. The top and bottom of each shelf were painted with high-gloss paint. The chrome edging is from the automotive section of the hardware store. It's used on trucks and cars, cuts easily with an X-Acto knife, and has a very sticky back. This was a fast and fun decorative touch.

step 1     *(Shot 1)* Prime both sides of the shelf and let it dry for 4 hours.

step 2     *(Shot 2)* Apply two coats of deep red latex paint to the top and bottom of the shelf, allowing each coat to dry for 4 hours.

step 3     *(Shot 3)* Make certain that the self-adhesive car trim is the same width as the shelf. Cut the trim to size. Remove the paper backing and press the trim on the edge of the shelf.

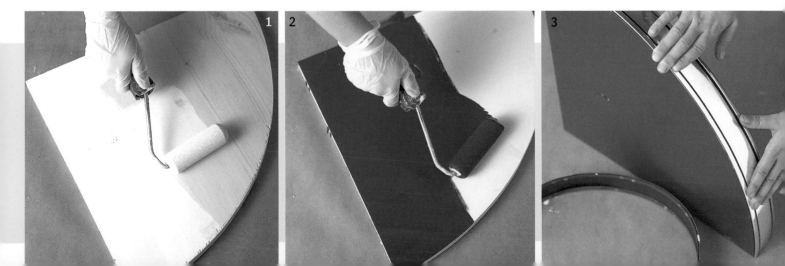

# back for basics

Great makeovers begin with a flash of inspiration, a burst of enthusiasm and energy, and a mad dash to the paint or hardware store. But the real work and the most important stage for any project is the preparation. Kitchens and bathrooms are both rooms that get constant use, so you will have to make alternative arrangements if they are going to be out of service for a while. Give yourself space and time to work and enjoy the process.

Once you have decided what projects you are undertaking, read through the instructions and make sure you have all the material and tools required. If it's a paint or plaster finish that you have never before attempted, then practice first on a board. I promise you, anyone can do the projects on these pages!

Even if your plans are small, it's important to clean and prepare the surfaces carefully so that your work will last. Paint will not stick to dirt, grease, or a slippery surface. Do a thorough cleanup with a heavy-duty cleanser such as trisodium phosphate (TSP). It is toxic, so wear gloves, plus a mask and goggles if you are sensitive. Rinse the surface free of the cleanser and wipe dry. Vinegar and hot water is an option if you prefer.

Sanding is the second step. As long as you will be using the correct primer for the job, it's not necessary to remove the old finish completely. But you need to sand enough to rough up the surface and give it tooth (something for the paint to stick to). To simplify this job there are small handheld electric sanders for large surfaces or sponge sanding blocks . The blocks are comfortable to hold, and the edges on the block make it easier to get into crevices and corners in cabinet molding. You can also wash the dust from the block and reuse it. If you are sanding wood, always rub in the direction of the grain.

Even when properly cleaned and sanded, a slippery surface such as plastic laminate requires a high-adhesive primer to complete the preparation stage. A good-quality primer will also be necessary if you are applying water-based paint over oil paint. Primers do several jobs. They seal plaster and wood in preparation for painting, and they block in stains or discoloration such as the knots in wood, which stops bleed through the base coat. High-adhesive primers are also the tooth that sits between the shiny surface on tile or laminates and the base coat of paint.

Paint comes in different qualities and sheens. Always use the best-quality paint you can afford. It will cover your surface better, you will need less, and it will last longer. Ceiling paint comes in a flat finish. It is not as strong as regular paint and is not meant to be used on walls. If you are doing a paint effect on the ceiling, use regular paint. The paint sheen is the degree of shininess your finish will have. A flat or matte finish will show fingerprints and is difficult to clean. A satin, velvet, or pearl sheen is the most common choice for walls as it is more forgiving, easily cleaned, and diminishes an uneven surface. Very durable semigloss is often used in kitchens and bathrooms. The glossier the paint, the more imperfections on the surface will show.

Varnish goes by many names: urethane, polyurethane, top coat. Water-based acrylic varnish looks milky in the can, but dries clear. Varnish also comes in a choice of sheens. If you want to ensure your paint or plaster effect is protected, it's worth the time to apply two coats of varnish. Let the first coat dry before applying the second.

A surface gets its sheen from the last coat of paint or varnish to go on. If you are varnishing on top of a paint effect, then the varnish sheen will count, not the paint sheen.

There are now ready-mixed stucco and plaster products available. Today stucco is generally not applied in such pointy or heavy textures. It can be rolled on like paint and left smooth or given a light texture. Venetian plaster comes in its natural off-white or pretinted, or you can tint it yourself. What makes it different is that marble dust has been mixed into the plaster. When you burnish the plaster (with a flattened metal spatula) the walls will shine and feel silky smooth. Concrete is appearing in contemporary kitchens and baths in the form of countertops, floors, and showers. Plasters and concrete are porous, and must be sealed to keep out dampness.

The pages that follow have the complete instructions for each of the basic projects seen in the kitchens and bathrooms throughout the book. A new style for your kitchen and bathroom will be dictated by budget and time. If both are ample, then do your homework well. If you decide on a quick fix-up, with fresh paint, plaster, and tile, then let your imagination soar, prepare your surfaces correctly, and choose colors and materials and finishes that you love.

# cabinets

Existing cabinets that are suitable for a makeover with paint are made from wood, wood laminate, and plastic laminate. One of the most common materials found in kitchens and bathrooms built or renovated over the last two decades is plastic laminate. Cabinets and countertops made from laminates are hardworking and tough, designed specifically to repel water, dirt, grease, fingerprints, and food stains. So it is no wonder that a coat of paint won't stick to it unless the surface is treated. Proper preparation includes thorough cleaning with a heavy-duty cleanser such as trisodium phosphate, sanding to rough up the surface, and a coat of a high-adhesive primer that is designed for slippery surfaces. Then you are ready to paint.

To get a professional paint finish, take down the cabinet doors and remove all the hardware. If you are going to replace the handles with new ones, try to match up the screw holes; old holes are difficult to camouflage successfully.

The style of the cabinet doors will suggest the type of paint finish that is most appropriate. Flat fronts are more conducive to modern effects such as solid colors or metal finishes. The flat-faced laminate door style with a wooden bar running along the bottom is the most common. We have repainted this style three different ways. See the Retro Reno kitchen on page 66, the Loft Life kitchen on page 70, and the New Shaker kitchen design on page 102.

Paneled cabinet doors lend themselves to antique finishes. The raised moldings can be highlighted or aged, with colors setting the tone and building atmosphere. There are many techniques for creating an antique finish, but the end result is the appearance of layers of paint that have been rubbed back by daily wear. See the Brick and Black kitchen on page 74.

# painting over plastic laminate

## MATERIALS AND TOOLS

*Heavy-duty cleanser such as TSP*

*Rubber kitchen gloves*

*Cleaning sponge or rag*

*Medium- and fine-grade sandpaper*

*High-adhesive primer*

*Low-pile roller and paint tray*

*Water-based (latex or acrylic) or oil paint or Hammerite*

*Satin acrylic varnish for water-based paint*

*Varnish brush or foam brush*

One of the most constantly asked questions I hear is if it's possible to paint over laminate cabinets (and counters; see page 164). Yes, it is not only possible, but you can transform any kitchen or bathroom with this simple task. Take the time to prepare your surfaces properly and the results will be stunning. If you use water-based paint, then you should apply varnish for protection. Low-sheen varnish is less durable, so apply three coats. Semigloss or gloss varnish is very durable, so one or two coats is plenty. Oil-based paint and Hammerite do not require a varnish top coat.

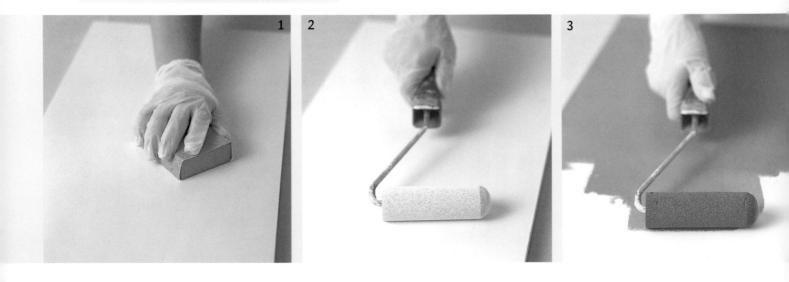

**step 1** Take down the cabinet doors and remove any hardware (handles and hinges). Use a sponge or rag to wash the surfaces to be painted with TSP. This heavy-duty cleanser will remove dirt and grease as well as some of the shine. It is recommended that you wear gloves for this. Rinse the surfaces and let them dry.

**step 2** *(Shot 1)* Sand the surface to give it tooth. Wipe off the sanding dust.

**step 3** *(Shot 2)* Apply a coat of high-adhesive primer with a low-pile roller and let it dry and cure overnight.

**step 4** *(Shot 3)* Apply two base coats of the paint of your choice. Water-based paint requires priming and also two to four coats of acrylic varnish, depending on sheen. Fine-grade sandpaper should be used for a light sanding between coats.

**step 5** *(Shots 4 and 5)* Hammerite paints are made for metal and come in hammered-effect, satin, or plain finishes. We have used the hammered-effect paint here, which goes on smooth, but as it dries, bumps will appear that imitate the look of battered metal. Hammerite is not to be used on countertops or any surface where food is prepared. Varnish is not required.

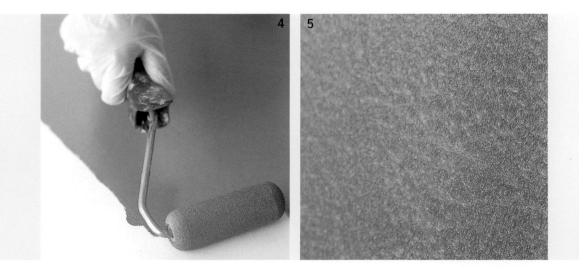

4    5

# milk paint on raw wood

## MATERIALS AND TOOLS

*Medium-grade sandpaper*

*Lint-free cloths*

*1-inch and 2-inch natural bristle paintbrushes*

*White or clear shellac*

*Cream milk paint*

*White candle*

*Russet red milk paint*

*Medium- and fine-grade steel wool*

Authentic milk paint comes in powder form and is mixed with water at home just prior to painting. Premixed milk paint is also available from specialty paint and craft stores. Rather than sitting on top of the wood's surface as regular paint does, milk paint sinks in and is absorbed by the wood's fibers. This durable paint was originally blended by the settlers in North America who used what resources they had close at hand. Colors were derived from natural sources, berries, roots, coal, and seeds. Latex paints are available in milk paint, heritage, or historic colors: subdued greens, blues, reds, browns, grays, black, and white. We used milk paint in the Quebec Cuisine kitchen on page 72. It is imperative that milk paint is applied to completely clean wood. All varnish, paint, and stain must be removed. The best results are on new, raw wood.

step 1  *(Shot 1)* Sand down the raw wood to open up the pores. Remove sanding dust with a rag.

step 2  *(Shot 2)* Use a 1-inch brush to cover the knots in the wood with clear shellac so the resins won't bleed through the paint.

step 3  *(Shot 3)* With the 2-inch brush, apply two coats of the cream base coat and let the paint dry for 4 hours.

step 4  *(Shot 4)* Rub white candle wax onto areas where the door would have naturally been worn down, such as along the edges and around the door handle. Rub in thin vertical patches.

step 5  *(Shot 5)* Paint the russet over the entire surface, including the waxed areas.

step 6  *(Shot 6)* Rub over the areas where you applied candle wax using the medium-grade steel wool. Because paint does not adhere to wax, the russet paint will come off to reveal the cream base coat.

step 7  Rub over the entire surface with fine steel wood to burnish it.

*Note:*  Milk paint does not require varnish.

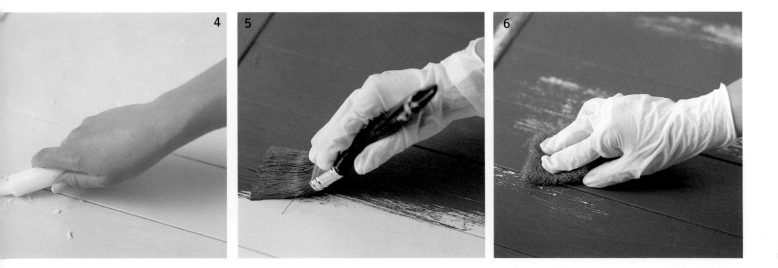

Finished wood cabinets require a light sanding to rough up the protective top coat, which is usually varnish. If the wood has been waxed, the wax will have to be removed before you prime or paint. (Use mineral spirits or Varsol and steel wool, and wear gloves.) Fill old screw holes and sand them flat, then prime the doors to ready them for their antique finish. In step 5 a damp rag is used to wipe back the black paint and reveal the red base coat because sandpaper can take away too much paint and you will expose the white primer.

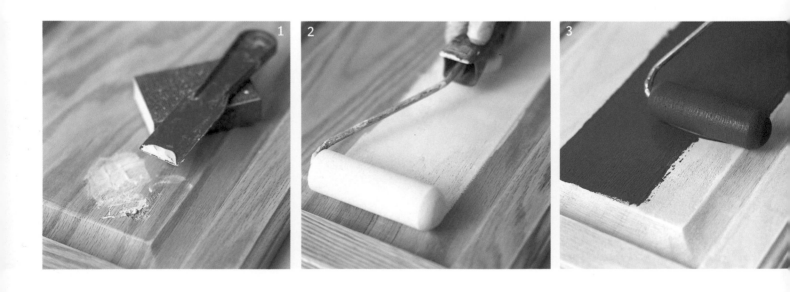

## MATERIAL AND TOOLS

*Wood filler (optional)*

*Medium-grade sandpaper*

*Lint-free cloths*

*High-adhesive primer*

*Low-pile rollers and paint trays*

*Red and black latex paint, low sheen*

*2½-inch paintbrush*

*Satin acrylic varnish*

*Varnish brush or foam brush*

step 1   *(Shot 1)* Repair any small cracks, nail holes, or screw holes (if you are changing the position of the hardware) with wood filler. Let it dry and then sand flush with the surface. Sand the surface to rough it up. Wipe off the sanding dust.

step 2   *(Shot 2)* Apply a coat of primer and let it dry for 4 hours.

step 3   *(Shot 3)* Roll on two coats of the red paint for complete coverage, allowing the first coat to dry before you apply the second coat.

step 4   *(Shot 4)* Dip the paintbrush into the black paint and remove most of the excess onto a rag. Dry-brush the black paint over the surface lightly. Build up the color, going into the indentations of the molding.

step 5   *(Shot 5)* Use a damp rag to wipe most of the black from the indentations, as well as some from areas on the door that would be naturally worn, to reveal the red base coat.

step 6   Apply one coat of varnish for protection.

# glazing wood cabinets

## MATERIALS AND TOOLS

*Coarse and medium-grade sandpa-
per, a sanding block, or a palm
sander*

*Mask (optional)*

*Paint stripper (optional)*

*Clean rags*

*Tack cloth (optional)*

*Water-based glazing liquid*

*Pale gray latex paint, satin*

*Mixing container*

*Thick sponge*

*Satin acrylic varnish*

*Varnish brush or foam brush*

I wanted to find a way to bring interest to an all-wood kitchen without losing the natural beauty of the wood (see Tasty Combination on page 106). The solution was to cover the cabinets with paint made translucent by mixing it with glazing liquid. The color of the wood changed, but you were still able to see the grain. The original varnish must be completely removed, a job made easier with a palm sander, or paint stripper if you prefer. Once the cabinets were prepared, I applied a thin coat of pale gray glaze with a sponge, always wiping in the direction of the grain. You can add a second coat if you prefer more opaque coverage. The surface must be varnished for protection.

step 1   *(Shot 1)* Sand down the wood to remove any varnish. For big jobs, it's advisable to wear a mask. You could use paint stripper first. Wipe the surface clean of any residue and sanding dust.

step 2   *(Shot 2)* Mix the pale gray glaze: 1 cup glazing liquid, ½ cup water, ¼ cup latex paint. Dip the sponge into the glaze and wipe over the surface, moving in the direction of the grain. Start with a thin coat, let dry, and add more if required. You should be able to see the wood's grain. Let the glaze dry thoroughly.

step 3   Apply two coats of varnish, allowing each coat to dry.

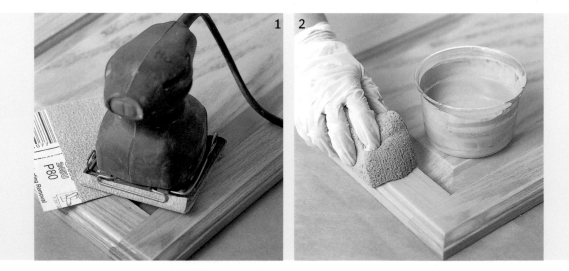

# antiquing old wood shutters

## MATERIALS AND TOOLS

*Terra-cotta and pale gray latex
    paint*

*2-inch paintbrush*

*Medium-grade sandpaper*

Sanding back layers of paint is the trick to this method of aging wood. In some places you can sand back as far as the natural wood. These shutters already had a few coats of white paint on them, and because of their age, I assumed it was oil-based paint. When you want to switch from oil to latex paint, you must apply a primer or the latex will not stick.

step 1   Apply the terra-cotta paint to the shutters, covering the old white paint or primer completely. Let the paint dry for 4 hours.

step 2   *(Shot 1)* Apply one coat of the gray paint and let it dry.

step 3   *(Shot 2)* Sand back through the gray to the terra-cotta paint along the edges of the wooden slats, along the edges of the frame, and in random areas along the flat surface of the shutters. If you like, rub back as far as the wood in some spots.

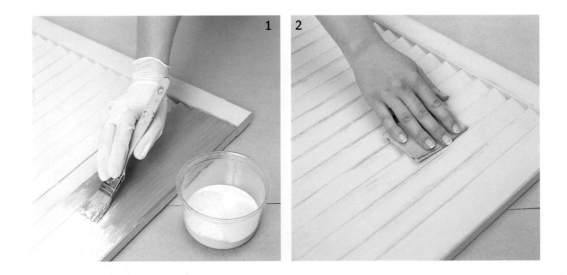

# tiles

For centuries tiles have been used as a decorative material for interior and exterior surfaces. For kitchens and bathrooms, the intrinsic beauty of stones such as granite, marble, and slate add a luxurious tone to walls, floors, and countertops. Terra-cotta and ceramic tiles share many of the same attributes as their more expensive cousins, but at a fraction of the price. Ceramic tiles are available in a variety of sizes, colors, and patterns with a matte or gloss finish. The surface may be flat or raised to form a pattern. Although handmade tiles created from terra-cotta, ceramic, or porcelain are costly, you can build your own custom look by placing them as accents within a plain ground. Mosaic tiles contribute to the most intricate of designs. Individualized patterns, such as the children's artwork seen on the backsplash on page 94, take time and patience to create but make a stunning focal point.

Although tiles are durable and water-resistant, the white grout that surrounds them does cause problems. In the bathroom the grout collects mold and mildew and discolors quickly. In the kitchen the grout is more difficult to keep clean and hygienic. One solution is to use colored or gray-tinted grout and to seal it with a proper grout sealer. This helps, but the sealer has to be reapplied every year or so.

If you want to change the color of existing tiles, painting is a short-term solution that works well. A proper primer designed to cover slippery surfaces must be applied over the tiles and grout. You will still see the tile demarcations as well as the pattern if one is embossed or raised on the tiles.

The tile on walls or floors can be completely camouflaged with special plaster or concrete. This produces an exciting new look that is very popular today. As with all finishes, it is mandatory to prepare the surface properly first and to follow the following steps in order to have a durable, long-lasting result. I do not recommend painting a tile floor.

# painting over ceramic tiles

## MATERIALS AND TOOLS

*Rubber or latex kitchen gloves*

*Cleaning sponge*

*Heavy-duty cleanser such as TSP*

*Lint-free cloths*

*Sandpaper or sanding block*

*High-adhesive primer*

*Low-pile rollers and paint trays*

*Oil or latex paint*

*Acrylic varnish*

*Varnish brush or foam brush*

One of the most common decorating dilemmas is facing a bathroom wall of tiles that are either an outdated color or just not your taste. Most likely the tiles are still in good shape, but the chocolate brown or the sunflower pattern isn't what you want. These tiles can be painted, even on the walls surrounding the bathtub. The surface must be scrubbed clean and a high-adhesive primer used. Water-based paint is fine as long as you seal it with two coats of acrylic varnish.

step 1   *(Shot 1)* Wearing gloves, use the sponge and cleanser to remove grease, dirt, and mildew from the tiles. Rinse and dry them with a lint-free cloth. Then go over the tiles with sandpaper or a sanding block to rough up the surface. Wipe off the sanding dust.

step 2   *(Shot 2)* Apply a coat of high-adhesive primer, making sure to cover all the grout and tile. Let the primer dry and cure overnight.

step 3   *(Shot 3)* Roll on the paint. Two coats is best, allowing the first coat to dry before applying the second. Apply two coats of varnish to seal and protect.

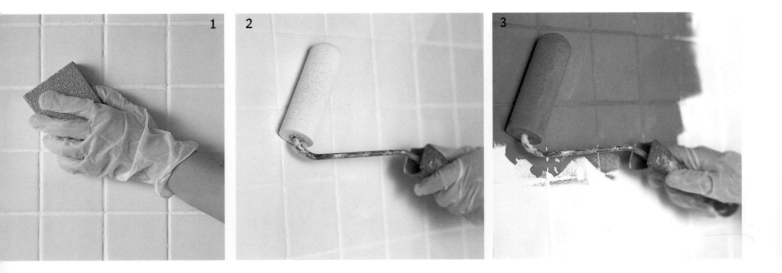

# applying stucco over tiled walls

## MATERIALS AND TOOLS

*Rubber or latex gloves*

*Cleaning sponge*

*Heavy-duty cleanser such as TSP*

*Etching cream*

*Wide paintbrush*

*Goggles and a mask*

*High-adhesive primer*

*Low-pile rollers and paint trays*

*Terra-cotta-tinted stucco*

*Burnt sienna powder pigment*

*Kitchen sponge*

*Red powder pigment*

*Varnish*

*3-inch roller*

Stucco, Venetian plaster, and concrete have made a big comeback in bathrooms and kitchens, but in an untraditional way. Here I used stucco to replicate terra-cotta tiles. They create not only the color required but also a more realistic texture than can be achieved with just paint. They can all be pretinted, which saves a step in the process. These new surfaces should be sealed to protect them from steam, water, dirt, and grease. I used Venetian plaster on the walls in the Mellow Yellow bath on page 134, and a special stucco for the tile walls in the Terra-Cotta Triumph bathroom on page 120 (instructions follow). These are ideal for the wall surface, but a stronger concrete must be used for the steps leading into a bathtub and on a floor. See page 160 for laying concrete over a tile floor.

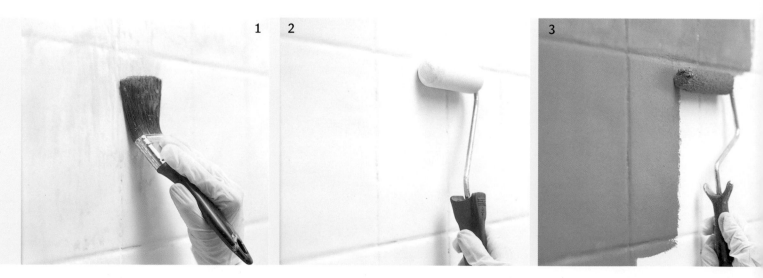

step 1   *(Shot 1)* Wearing gloves, use the sponge and cleanser to wash the surface thoroughly. Rinse and dry it. Following the directions on the bottle, apply a thick coat of the etching cream to the tiles with the wide paintbrush. Wear protective gloves, goggles, and a mask as it is a corrosive material. The etching cream removes the sheen from the tiles to make them more adhesive. Rinse the etching cream off the walls and dry them.

step 2   *(Shot 2)* Apply a coat of high-adhesive primer using the roller, making sure to cover the grout as well. Let it dry overnight.

step 3   *(Shot 3)* Pour the terra-cotta-colored stucco into a small tray and roll it onto the wall as evenly as possible. Let it dry for 4 hours, then roll on a second coat. Try to avoid making roller marks. Cover the grout lines as well (but their indentations will still be visible).

step 4   *(Shot 4)* Always wear a mask when mixing powders. Mix 1 tablespoon of burnt sienna powder pigment with 1 cup of water. Dip the clean kitchen sponge into the colored water and dab it randomly over the surface to create a mottled effect. It will dry quickly and soak into the stucco, but as long as you keep it wet, you can continue to move the color around, removing some or adding more.

Dip the kitchen sponge into the dry red powder pigment and dab it sparingly onto the wall around the brown areas, just to highlight them and the terra-cotta color underneath.

step 5   *(Shot 5)* Let the surface dry overnight and then apply two coats of varnish using a roller. Water-based varnish goes on milky and dries clear.

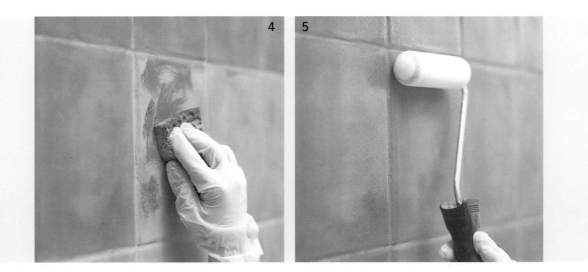

# concrete over floor tile

One of the most dramatic transformations we have performed on *The Painted House* is thanks to the application of a decorative concrete over existing floor tiles. Witness the stunning results in the French Twist bathroom on page 110. Because the shiny tiles have to be dulled in order for the concrete to adhere, there is some work involved. The most successful way to proceed is with etching cream, which is brushed over the tiles thickly, left to work for 4 or 5 minutes, and then scraped off. Care must be taken when handling the cream; it is very corrosive. Wear a mask, eye goggles, and gloves and work in a well-ventilated area. Once the etching cream is removed and the surface washed clean of any residue, then a bonder is rolled on. Now the concrete will adhere well, so you can enjoy your new floor for years to come.

## MATERIALS AND TOOLS

*Gloves, goggles, and mask*

*Etching cream*

*Paintbrush*

*Cleaning sponge*

*Clean rags*

*Cement bonder or high-adhesive primer*

*Low-pile roller and paint tray*

*Metal spatulas*

*Cement tinted to a limestone shade (see Resources*

*Ruler*

1  2

step 1   *(Shot 1)* Working in a well-ventilated area and wearing protective gloves, goggles, and a mask, brush the etching cream over the floor tiles. Let it sit for 4 or 5 minutes, then remove the cream and rinse the tiles thoroughly with a cleaning sponge. Wipe them dry. This step removes the glossy finish on the tiles.

step 2   *(Shot 2)* Apply a bonder with a roller to allow better adhesion between the cement and the tiles. Let it dry overnight.

step 3   *(Shot 3)* Use a metal spatula to apply the first skim coat of cement to the tiles, filling in the grout lines. Let it dry overnight.

step 4   *(Shot 4)* Apply a second coat to the entire surface. The idea is to have a completely flat surface with all the original grout lines hidden. Make the surface as smooth as possible.

step 5   *(Shot 5)* Let the second coat dry for a couple of hours, until it is just hard, and then score the cement with a ruler and metal spatula, replicating limestone blocks. Let the cement dry thoroughly. Check the product directions for sealing instructions.

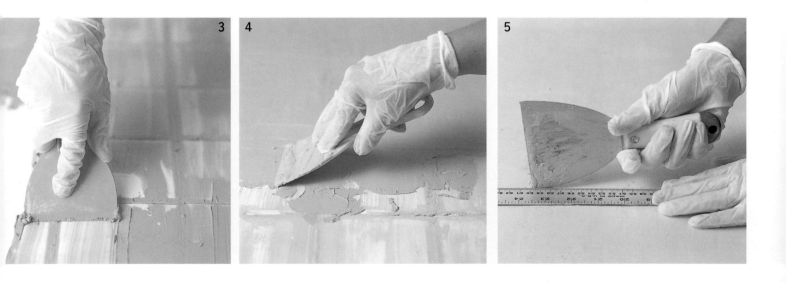

# painting loose ceramic tiles

The backsplash area in the kitchen or bath is a perfect place to create a focal point. You can do this easily and at little cost by making a custom design and painting the inexpensive white tiles yourself. In this kitchen we applied the tiles on the diagonal to break up the linear motion of the cupboards. Ceramic paint is available at art and craft stores. Generally these paints are meant to be baked in the oven in order to cure the colors, so they are not an option for tiles that are already installed on the wall.

## MATERIALS AND TOOLS

*White ceramic tiles, matte finish*
*1-inch paintbrush*
*Ceramic paint in your choice of colors*
*Baking sheet*

step 1    *(Shot 1)* Clean the tiles thoroughly to get rid of any dust or dirt. Dip the paintbrush into the paint and brush it onto the tile, always brushing in the same direction. Don't worry about brush marks. They add an appealing naïve quality to the painting.

step 2    *(Shot 2)* Preheat the oven to the temperature recommended by the brand of ceramic paint you are using. Place the painted tiles on a baking sheet and bake for the prescribed length of time.

step 3    Allow the tiles to cool completely before applying them to the wall with tile glue.

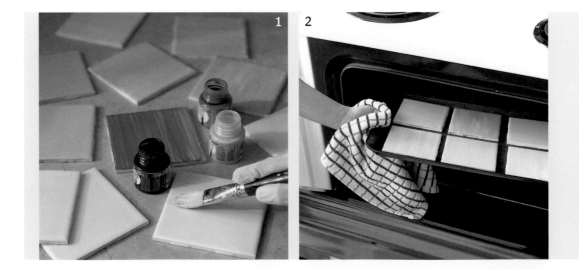

# cutting and painting glass and mirror

## MATERIALS AND TOOLS

*Large board*

*3 small pieces of wood*

*Finishing nails and hammer*

*Heavy-duty work gloves and goggles*

*Marker*

*Ruler*

*Mirror tiles*

*Glass cutter*

*Sanding block*

*Glass paint*

*3-inch plastic spatula*

*Small plate*

It's not difficult to cut glass or mirror as long as you have the proper tool. A glass cutter is available at hardware and specialty art and craft stores. One end of the tool is used to score and cut the glass and the other is shaped to rap the glass after you have scored it to make a clean cut. A little practice and you'll have it. You can cut pieces of mirror into tiles for a unique backsplash as we have done here for the Retro Reno kitchen on page 66.

step 1    *(Shot 1)* With the board and small blocks of wood and nails, build a jig as shown in photo to make measuring and cutting easier. The mirror squares will be 3 inches. Always wear work gloves and goggles when cutting and handling the broken mirror.

step 2    *(Shot 2)* Set tile in jig and mark off the cutting line with the ruler and marker. Score the mirror with the glass cutter along the mark. Press down hard and go over the line once.

step 3    *(Shot 3)* Cut the 3-inch lengths first and then go back and cut the lengths into squares.

step 4    *(Shot 4)* Once a line has been scored, there are two ways to break the glass. Use the other end of the cutter and hit the score line, or hold the glass on either side of the scored line and snap. Sand the sharp edges.

step 5    *(Shot 5)* Pour the glass paint into the plate. It is quite thick, like a gel, so it should go on quite smoothly with the spatula. A brush would leave brush strokes. Let dry, then bake according to the manufacturer's instructions.

# painting over a plastic laminate counter

## MATERIAL AND TOOLS

*Rubber or latex gloves*

*Heavy-duty cleanser such as TSP*

*Cleaning sponge*

*Sandpaper or sanding block*

*Lint-free cloth*

*Low-tack painter's tape*

*High-adhesive primer*

*Small foam rollers and trays*

*White, black, brown, and light gray latex paint*

*Sea sponges*

*Paper toweling*

*Acrylic varnish and foam brush (optional)*

The work surface around the sink in the kitchen and bathroom takes a lot of wear and tear. It must be water, heat, and stain resistant, and easy to clean and disinfect on a daily basis. Quite often the material used for countertops is a plastic laminate. Laminate counters can be renewed with paint as a short-term solution to update your room. The preparation is the same as for laminate cabinets—thorough cleaning, sanding and priming. Then you can paint the countertop a solid color; see the fresh, white counter in the country kitchen on page 29 and the russet red counter that perks up a rental kitchen on page 84. Or try a paint finish such as faux granite, shown here and in the Brick and Black kitchen on page 74. The results are so realistic, this homeowner thought we had replaced his old counter with real granite. For latex paint, apply three or four coats of acrylic varnish. Let the counter dry and cure for a week before using it. Although it will feel dry to the touch, it takes longer for the paint to harden into a tough durable finish.

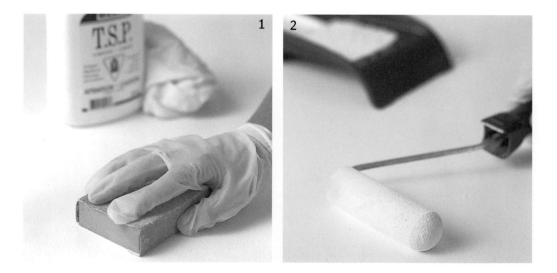

1  2

step 1   (*Shot 1*) Wearing gloves, clean the counter with TSP. Rinse and dry it with a sponge. Sand the surface lightly to rough it up. Wipe it with a clean cloth. Tape off the wall surrounding the countertop with low-tack tape to protect it from the paint.

step 2   (*Shot 2*) Apply one coat of high-adhesive primer and let it dry. Apply one coat of white paint with a roller. Let dry.

step 3   (*Shot 3 and Shot 4*) Rip a sea sponge into pieces that fit into the palm of your hand. Use a separate piece of sea sponge for each color. Dab the first sponge into the black paint, take off the excess paint using a paper towel and then dab the color onto the counter, leaving some areas of white showing. Fill in more with the brown paint, then a bit of gray; alternate back and forth until you are satisfied with the effect. The sea sponge gives the paint the speckled look you find in granite.

step 4   (*Shot 5*) Add three coats of varnish for protection.

# concrete island

Concrete is appearing more and more in finished interiors, from floors in lofts to kitchen countertops and bathroom showers. It is not the same product that you see on sidewalks. There are binders added to make it crack resistant. Concrete is porous, so requires a sealant to make it waterproof and easy to clean. There are different products on the market, and different brand names. Check with your hardware or paint professional and read the instructions on the label to be sure that you have the right product for the job. As a solid base, concrete is very heavy, but it can be applied as a thin coat over most existing surfaces.

The original island in the Retro Reno kitchen on page 66 was built from plywood and white laminate. We replaced the top with a stainless steel counter and applied concrete patch to the sides. A solid concrete island would have been expensive and far too heavy, but I got the look of solid concrete by applying concrete and mortar patch over the laminate. It is now a modern structure that suits the new steel appliances and turquoise painted cabinets.

## MATERIALS AND TOOLS

Rubber or latex gloves

Sandpaper or sanding block

Clean rags

Spatula

Gray concrete and mortar patch

Sea sponge

Setting compound (such as Durabond compound powder)

Gray latex paint, satin

Aluminum powder

Mask

Oil-based satin varnish

Varnish brush or foam brush

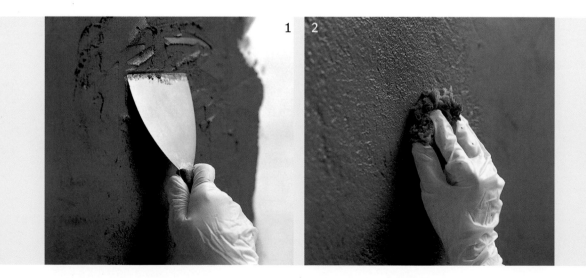

**step 1** *(Shot 1)* Sand the laminate to rough up the surface. Wipe the surface with a clean rag. Using the spatula, apply a ⅛-inch-thick coat of the gray concrete to cover the entire surface.

**step 2** *(Shot 2)* Let the concrete dry for about 15 minutes, then dab the concrete with a damp sponge to pit it, giving it some texture. Let the concrete dry thoroughly; it should feel dry and be a uniform color. Overnight is best.

**step 3** *(Shot 3)* Mix the setting compound according to the directions on the package, then to each cup of compound add 3 tablespoons of gray paint and 1 tablespoon of aluminum powder. Always wear a mask when mixing metallic powders, as they are toxic. With the spatula apply a thin coat of the paint mixture over the surface. Let it dry for 2 hours, or until completely dry.

**step 4** *(Shot 4)* Wearing a mask, sand over the surface lightly to let some of the base coat show through and to soften some of the bigger peaks. Wipe off any excess sanding dust.

**step 5** *(Shot 5)* Apply two coats of oil-based varnish. This will add depth to the finish as well as seal it.

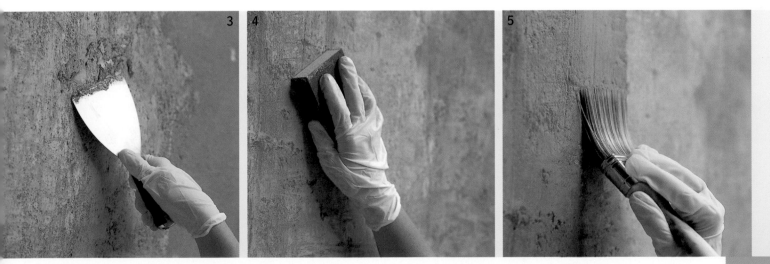

# walls

## painting horizontal stripes

**MATERIALS AND TOOLS**

*All-purpose primer (optional)*

*Bright white latex paint*

*Low-pile roller and tray*

*Pencil and ruler*

*Chalk line*

*Level*

*1-inch low-tack painter's tape*

*Bright white and indigo blue latex paint*

*Small roller and paint tray*

*Clean rag*

When you want to add a bit of pizzazz to a tiny bathroom, a roll of tape and a bright color will fix you up in no time. See the True Blue bathroom on page 124. Stripes are a great decorating tool since our eyes follow their direction. Vertical stripes make walls seem higher while horizontal stripes widen a room and make it feel more spacious. You can choose a width that divides equally into the area you are working on and fill the stripes with either solid paint or a paint finish such as colorwashing. Stripes exaggerate flaws in a wall surface such as cracks or bumps, where the lines will not be straight. For quick measuring and marking, enlist the aid of a friend to hold one end of the chalk line.

step 1   Apply two coats of the white base coat and let it dry for at least 4 hours or overnight.

step 2   *(Shot 1)* Start from the ceiling down, and divide the wall into even sections approximately 10 inches wide. Measure and mark first with a ruler and pencil so that you have points down the edges of both walls as guides, then press the chalk line taut against the guide marks and ping the line. (This is when you need two people.) Use a level to make sure the lines are straight.

step 3   *(Shot 2)* Tape along the outside of every other stripe. Press down firmly so that you get a clean line. Apply two coats of the blue paint with a roller. Allow the first coat to dry for 4 hours before applying the second coat.

step 4   *(Shot 3)* Remove the tape after the second coat and let the paint dry overnight. Wipe off any chalk residue with a damp cloth.

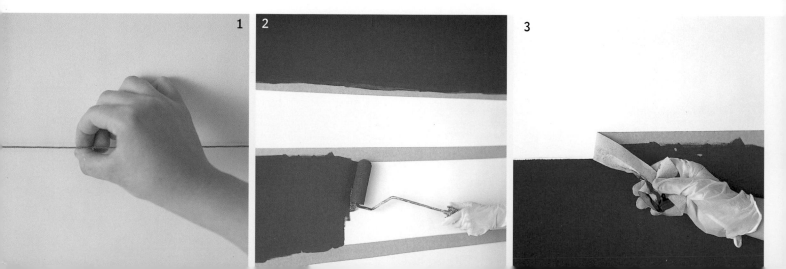

# colorwashing

## MATERIAL AND TOOLS

*Cream latex paint*

*Low-pile roller and paint tray*

*Raw sienna and burnt sienna latex paint or artist's acrylics*

*2 mixing containers*

*Stir sticks*

*Low-tack painter's tape*

*Clean soft rags*

## GLAZE RECIPES

*Using latex paint*

*1 part latex paint*

*2 parts glazing liquid*

*Using artist's acrylics*

*Approximately 2 teaspoons artist's acrylic paint*

*4 cups water-based glazing liquid*

Colorwashing is one of the most popular paint techniques. It covers a myriad of sins and works with most colors. One of my favorite combinations is a blend of terra-cotta shades. You can use latex paint, but for a purer color, try mixing artist's acrylics into glazing liquid. Both recipes are listed below. When applying any paint effect that needs to be worked, glazing liquid slows down the drying time so you have time to "play" with the paint. Work in sections and keep a wet edge so that you won't get lap lines. If the paint has dried by the time you get back to it, roller on a bit of clear glaze to open it up again. For these kitchen walls, shown in the Elements of the Kitchen, on page 14, I first applied a cream base coat, which peeks through the colored glazes, creating many soft layers of terra-cotta.

step 1    Apply two base coats of cream paint, allowing the first coat to dry before adding the second.

step 2    In separate containers, using stir sticks, mix the ingredients for the light- and dark-colored glazes. Stir well. You will colorwash one wall at a time. Taping off the edges so that you don't get a buildup of paint in the corners, apply the paint effect to sections of approximately 3 × 3 feet, as follows.

step 3    *(Shot 1)* Dip the end of a damp rag into the paler glaze and rub it over the first section in random patches, just like washing a wall. Leave some spots bare.

step 4    *(Shot 2)* Fill in some of the bare spots by rubbing on the darker glaze.

step 5    *(Shot 3)* Dab and blend the two colors together with a clean rag folded flat. Move to the next section and work the wet edge first so that you don't get lap lines.

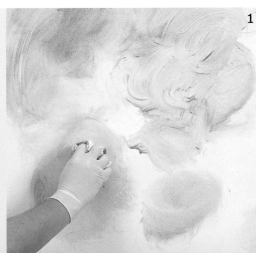

1    2

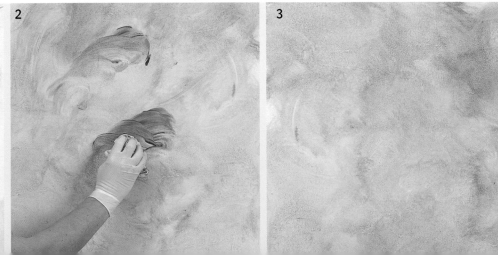

3

# venetian plaster walls

## MATERIALS AND TOOLS

*High-adhesive primer*

*Low-pile roller and paint tray*

*Venetian plaster*

*Metal spatulas or plaster trowels*

*Gold metallic gel or gold glaze*

*Satin acrylic varnish*

*Varnish brush or foam brush*

Venetian plaster is very exciting to work with, and it is not difficult to apply. Work over primed walls. Use two trowels, one to scoop the plaster from the bucket and the other to then transfer that scoop onto. Scrape the plaster onto the wall in thin skim coats. Pull the trowel down the wall, then across in what is called a cross-hatch motion. The idea is to leave behind a mostly smooth coat, with just a hint of texture. What makes Venetian plaster so special is that it has marble dust in it. Over the final coat of dry plaster hold the spatula flat against the wall and burnish the plaster to bring up a silky shine. You can leave some areas matte and burnish others to create depth and brilliance. Plaster walls feel luxurious. Venetian plaster is a lovely off-white color to begin with. It can be tinted, but for this project we left it in its natural color. See the walls in the Mellow Yellow bathroom on page 134. A metallic gel is applied between two skim coats of plaster, which creates a gorgeous shading and depth.

step 1   *(Shot 1)* Prime the walls and let them dry overnight. Apply a thin skim coat of plaster with the spatula, so thin you can see some areas of the primer showing. Use a cross-hatch motion, applying the plaster in one direction and then another. You want only a very subtle texture left behind. Let the plaster dry.

step 2   *(Shot 2)* Apply the gold gel in the same manner as the plaster skim coat. Smear the gel with the spatula over and across the plaster to highlight the subtle texture underneath. Let it dry.

step 3   *(Shot 3)* Veil over the top with a second coat of thinly applied plaster. It should be a skim coat that shows the tones of white, while allowing bits of gold gel to shimmer through. Let this layer dry overnight.

step 4   Because this is a bathroom, you should apply two coats of acrylic varnish to seal.

1

2

3

# tinted stucco walls

## MATERIALS AND TOOLS

*High-adhesive primer*

*Low-pile roller and paint tray*

*Pretinted blue, red, and desert sand stucco or plain stucco and universal tints*

*Mixing containers*

*Stir sticks*

*Small- and medium-size metal trowels*

*Acrylic varnish and foam brush (optional)*

In the High Sierra Powder Room on page 138, I applied three colors of stucco to create the effect of walls that have been plastered and baked by the hot sun over many decades. Small amounts of the vivid blue and red are spread randomly over the walls first, and then a skim coat of the desert sand brown is troweled over the top, allowing bits of color to peek through. The stucco needs to be applied in thin layers or it will crack. It has a matte finish and cannot be burnished like Venetian plaster as it lacks the marble dust. Seal stucco walls in a bathroom with two coats of varnish.

Unlike paint, which dries darker, stucco dries about 50 percent lighter, so it's a good idea to experiment on a board until you get the colors you want. You can add color to the stucco on your own by mixing in universal tints, or the paint store can do this for you.

step 1   Prime the walls and let them dry overnight. If you are doing your own coloring, divide the plaster into separate containers. Add the tints a little at a time and mix well.

step 2   *(Shot 1)* Apply the bright blue and red plasters to the wall in random patches with a small metal trowel. You need only a small amount on the edge of your trowel, then scrape downward.

step 3   *(Shot 2)* With the larger trowel, apply a rough skim coat of the sand plaster over the surface, allowing colored patches to show through. All plaster dries lighter. Play with the effect until you are satisfied. You can add more colors or cover up with the sand.

step 4   For a bathroom, you should apply two coats of acrylic varnish to seal.

1   2

# resources

Debbie Travis Specialty Collections—a line of specialty products such as glaze, suede paint, stone-finish stucco, and more, for the contemporary, elegant interior. Available through the Painted House website, www.painted-house.com, or by calling our toll-free number, 1-800-932-3446. Also through Martin & Associates, 1-800-204-6278.

Kitchen designer for pages 8 and 21
Architem
Montreal, Quebec

Designer for kitchen and bathroom, pages 15 and 61
Jean Francois Menard
Atelier Auguste
Montreal, Quebec
(514) 485-1920

Designer for kitchen on page 44
Christine Shannon of Ivory Moon

Designer for bathroom on page 62
Jolie Korek
Interiors Company, Inc.
Scarsdale, New York

Designer for kitchen on page 65
Anne Cote
Art Director for *Debbie Travis' Facelift* television series

Cork floors, pages 37, 65, 136 and laminate floors on pages 36, 81
Torlys
Canada
1-800-461-2573
www.torlys.com

Waterworks bathroom products, pages 47, 51, 57, 59
United States
1-800-998-BATH
www.waterworks.com, or
contactus@waterworks.com
Canada
Distributed by: Ginger's Bath Centre
1-888-444-3292
www.elte.com

Elte Carpets and Home
Canada
1-888-444-3292
www.elte.com

Glass Paint, pages 68 and 163, ceramic paint, page 162
Pebeo
Available at art supply stores around the world.
www.pebeo.com

One of the designers who helped to create the kitchen on page 88 and bathroom on page 130
Mazyar Mortazavi
TAS Designbuild
Canada
(416) 510-8181
www.tasdesignbuild.com

Pages 89, 97 and 107
Richelieu Hardware
Head Office
Ville St-Laurent, Quebec
(514) 336-4144 www.richelieu.com

Faux brick paneling, page 95
Available at home renovation centers.

Mosaic backsplash, pages 93 and 94
Mosaic kits available at art and craft supply stores.
Mosaic artist, Laura Edell.

Hammerite paint, pages 98, 149
Available at good paint supply stores and home renovation centers.
www.hammerite.com

Rubber floor, page 98
Canada & U.S.
American Biltrite
1-800-479-0190
flooring@american-biltrite.com,
www.american-biltrite.com

Pressed metal backsplash, pages 107, 108, 109
Canada
Steptoe & Wife Antiques
1-800-461-0060
info@steptoewife.com,
www.steptoewife.com
United States
Shanker Industries Inc. (516) 766-6655
sales@shanko.com, www.shanko.com

Corian countertop, page 107
For a distributor near you visit the website, www.corian.com

Stamped ceiling, page 112
Stamps widely available at art and craft stores.

Decorative concrete floor, pages 113, 160
Jewel Stone
DuRock Textured Protective Coatings
Toll free 1-888-238-6345
(905) 856-0133
www.durock.com

Stucco, pages 122, 158, Venetian plaster, pages 138, 139, 170, metallic gel, page 138, 170
Texturline
U.S. & Canada, 1-800-773-5233
www.texturline.com

Silver leaf, page 128
Available at specialty art and craft supply stores.

Self-bonding concrete, pages 132, 134
Available at hardware and some paint stores.

Frosted glass spray paint, page 137
Available at home renovation centers and art and craft supply stores.

Automotive trim, page 143
At auto parts and detailing shops.

Green painter's tape
Tape Specialties
Tel: 1-800-463-8273
Fax: (905) 669-2330
www.thegreentape.com
tape.specialties@sympatico.ca

Additional Photography Credits
Photographs on pages 18, 19, 24, top left 29, top left 32, top left 33, 45, 48, 53, 54, 55 are © magazine/IPC Syndication. Photographs on pages 25, 26, 27, courtesy Sub Zero. Photographs on pages 58, top left 61, courtesy Hotel Place d'Armes, Montreal, Quebec, Canada. Photograph on page 11, Joe Oliveira. Photographs on pages 71 and 156, Peter Sellar. Photographs on pages 107, 108, 109, Ernst Hellrung.

# index

Page numbers in *italics* indicate illustration captions.